The Diplomatic Art

THE
DIPLOMATIC
ART

*An informal history
of world diplomacy*

Charles Roetter

MACRAE SMITH COMPANY:
PHILADELPHIA

Contents

CONTENTS

6

"Diplomacy is easy on the brain but hell on the feet."

CHARLES G. DAWES, former United States Ambassador to the Court of St. James's in London.

"It depends on which you use."

HENRY PRATHER FLETCHER, former United States Ambassador to Italy, commenting on Charles G. Dawes' remark.

The Diplomatic Art

1:

Diplomacy in the Nuclear Age

DIPLOMACY IS THE ART OF NEGOTIATION BETWEEN sovereign states. Its practice varies from generation to generation.

In 1779, Lord Malmesbury, Britain's ambassador to the Court of St. Petersburg, was considered to have scored a major diplomatic triumph when the Empress Catherine received him in her private dressing room—alone. Malmesbury was an exceptionally handsome man, and in his dispatch home he reported that the susceptible Empress— who was at that time well over fifty—told him, "Were I a younger woman, I might be less prudent."

There were no raised eyebrows in London, no calls

for an investigation into Foreign Office methods. On the contrary, Whitehall was delighted. Anglo-Russian relations had never seemed so cordial.

Nowadays Whitehall holds the view that the presence of one of Her Majesty's ambassadors in a lady's private dressing room does not advance Britain's cause. Nor are ambassadors to Russia—or anywhere else for that matter —picked for the qualities which obviously led to Lord Malmesbury's choice.

The explanation is simple: there is today no lady whose dressing room can compare in influence with Catherine the Great's. Power is more diffuse, and so boudoir diplomacy has died a natural death, killed by the forward march of democracy and the concept that all men—and women —are, or ought to be, equal.

Instead of a craft practiced by a select few, diplomacy has become an expanding mass industry. There is more of it than ever before.

International affairs are still largely played against the ornate background of Louis Quinze furniture, but the telegraph, the telephone and the airplane have changed the tempo. And the development of rockets and nuclear weapons within the last generation has dramatically raised the price of failure. A third world war could mean not only the destruction of countless cities and vast tracts of land but the end of civilized existence on this planet. The stakes in the diplomatic game have never been higher.

It is small wonder, therefore, that international relations nowadays seem to be conducted at a fast and furious pace. There are two main power blocs, one of which believes with fanatical fervor not only that it possesses in

Communism a cure for all the world's ills but also that it has the right, nay the duty, to prescribe and administer that cure to everyone everywhere. It employs all means short of total war because, after lengthy debate, even Moscow has at last officially recognized the fact that total war in the nuclear age is a form of self-destruction. The trouble is that no one is absolutely certain just how and why a total war could start. The demarcation line between the two power blocs is defined clearly in only very few places, notably in Central Europe and along the thirty-eighth parallel in Korea. The rest of the world—and the rest includes many parts of Europe, the whole of Africa and substantial sections of Asia and Latin America—is treated as a sort of Tom Tiddler's ground. Consequently no diplomat can afford to assess the importance of any event there in purely local terms. A revolution in Latin America? Religious strife in the Middle East? A political assassination in darkest Africa? They affect us all. We have indeed, whether we like it or not, become One World.

Lord Palmerston conducted the nation's foreign affairs by coming up to London from Broadlands in Hampshire for two or three days a week, and the handful of languid young gentlemen who served at the Foreign Office whiled away the hours by flashing mirrors at the Prime Minister's housemaids at No. 10 Downing Street—until Lord Palmerston issued instructions that even when there was no work to be done, they were "not to cast reflections on the ladies across the road."

That age has passed. Modern Foreign Secretaries are surrounded by batteries of telephones and hordes of keen, hard-working experts capable of advising them on subjects as diverse as tribal customs in the South Seas or soil erosion in the Middle East. The monthly trickle of handwritten dispatches coming into their offices has become a daily torrent of telegrams.

In Lord Palmerston's day, Britain maintained only three embassies abroad—in St. Petersburg, in Paris and in Vienna. Elsewhere a resident Minister with a staff of two or three clerks was thought sufficient. Today, even Luxembourg is graced by the presence of one of Her Britannic Majesty's ambassadors, and among his staff are to be found an Army, an Air and a Commercial Attaché.

Not that the ever-expanding network of embassies and legations can be held entirely responsible for the increase in diplomats. The sovereign remedy prescribed for every international ailment nowadays is this: when in doubt, hold a conference; when at a loss, set up an international organization.

In the old days, up-and-coming towns built cathedrals. Today, they build conference halls, install new telephone exchanges and lengthen the runways of their airports in order to attract international organizations. Fortunately, there are plenty to go round.

New York has the UN; Strasbourg, the Council of Europe; Washington, the Organization of American States; London, Western European Union; Brussels, the headquarters of the European Common Market; Rome, the World Health Organization; Geneva, the Economic Commission for Europe; Bangkok, the South-East Asia Treaty Organization; Luxembourg, the Coal and Steel Pool; Paris, NATO, General Lemnitzer's Supreme Allied Headquarters and UNESCO. Paris also has Interpol. And there is no need for other towns to despair. Plans for a number of new international bodies are at present being actively considered.

In view of this trend, it is perhaps not surprising that some countries are fast running out of diplomats. Iceland gave up the unequal struggle long ago. Its representation on a number of international organizations dealing with defense, social matters, economics and culture in the Western hemisphere is in the hands of one solitary diplomat. But then, of course, no matter what the context of the meeting or the agenda, Iceland is concerned with only one question—herrings.

Countries whose national requirements are less simple cannot take this easy way out. They occasionally call on businessmen, bankers, lawyers, soldiers, professors, playwrights and philanthropists to help out the overworked career men.

Politicians, too, are increasingly tempted to try their hand at the diplomatic game. After the "summit" meeting in Geneva, whole planeloads of United States Congressmen and Senators disappeared behind the Iron Curtain, each one a self-appointed ambassador determined to "see for himself." On his return, after a lightning tour through the satellite countries and Russia, one of them gave it as his considered opinion that his trip had been "a revelation, different from the impression I had gained from the State Department." At a farm in Southern Rumania, he explained, he had eaten "bread and cheese, the finest tomatoes you could imagine, chicken soup, fried chicken, eggplant, tea, cheesecake and fried watermelon. The chicken had been fried Southern style. It was so good I sucked every

15

bone. When I got up from that table, I was so bloated, I could hardly walk."

Another touring legislator described Mr. Krushchev as "the closest thing they have got to a regular guy."

No doubt Metternich, Talleyrand and Castlereagh would have been appalled at this way of conducting affairs between nations. Even Benjamin Franklin, a sturdy democrat, would have raised a disapproving eyebrow. Certainly James Monroe could never have negotiated the Louisiana Purchase, which enabled the United States to expand westwards to the Pacific Ocean, if his elbow had been constantly jogged by junketing Senators.

But the modern diplomat must learn to work with, and under, politicians whose sole aim in life is to please a fickle electorate. If ever the thought should strike him that the whims of a capricious empress could perhaps be preferable to the unpredictable enthusiasms of a sovereign people's elected representatives, he will keep his doubts to himself. For him, these intrusions are all part and parcel of modern diplomacy's complex pattern—together with such recent innovations as press curiosity, klieg lights, microphones and television cameras.

Yet, although the old, traditional ways are being swept aside, there still clings to diplomats, even today, a slightly sinister aura of Machiavellian mystery. Nobody is really quite certain what these fellows in "striped pants" are up to. There seem to be more of them every month, but just how do they spend their days? What lies behind the noncommital smiles and the studiously platitudinous communiqués which appear to be all that ever emerges from their mammoth conferences?

16

Half the population of Britain and America look upon the Foreign Office and State Department as citadels of reaction, and the other half as hotbeds of revolution.

In their own mind's eye, diplomats are imperturbable, courteous, painstaking, capable of seeing all sides of a problem and firm or conciliatory, depending on the situation. In the view of many members of the general public, they are callous, cynical, standoffish, indolent, superficial, supercilious and vacillating.

The only time an ordinary mortal is ever likely to suspect that there beats a heart behind the smooth exterior, that there may, in fact, even lurk a temper, is in the early hours of the morning after an overnight transatlantic flight. Waiting for his turn outside the crowded washroom, unshaven, even the most polished diplomat finds it difficult to be suave.

It would be wrong to suggest, however, that the public image of diplomats is the same in every detail throughout the world. There are subtle shades of difference here and there. Most Britons, for instance, are convinced that they have a natural flair for diplomacy and that one of the most valuable contributions that the island race is making to the Western Alliance is its long experience and traditional expertise in this field. By contrast, many Americans believe that an American diplomat, no matter how highly trained he may be, can at any time be talked into buying the diplomatic equivalent of Brooklyn Bridge by any and every smooth, silver-tongued European ambassador. They delight in examples of American diplomatic failures, and ignore the fact that American diplomats in most cases are perfectly capable of holding their own.

Of course, many ambassadors nowadays have learned the value of good public relations, and spare no effort to put themselves and the importance of their jobs across to the general public.

For instance, Mrs. Clare Boothe Luce, for many years the United States Ambassador in Rome, tried to see all the thousands of American tourists who arrived in the Eternal City with letters of introduction from friends of friends of friends.

"During the heavy season," she once explained, "I try to set aside a half hour between four and five in the afternoon which I call my catch-all time. I go out into the lobby, and shake hands with anyone who wants to see me."

Someone put it to her that the procedure she had adopted was rather reminiscent of an audience with the Pope, but she was not in the least nonplussed. "With this difference," she replied, "the Pope gives people his blessing, while I hope the people in the lobby will give me one."

Certainly the advent of the nuclear age has sharpened public interest in diplomats and their work as never before. For every crisis nowadays raises the awesome specter of complete annihilation, and in times of international tension the world anxiously watches the comings and goings of ambassadors, foreign ministers, presidents and prime ministers. We argue about the United Nations and its Secretary General. We wonder whether a "summit" meeting would help and how far personalities matter. We try to assess the chances of fruitful negotiation, speculate about what the Russians are up to, and ask whether the traditional concepts of old-fashioned diplomacy have not had their day. Above all, we hope that the important-looking men hurrying in and out of the White House, the United Nations buildings, No. 10 Downing Street or the Kremlin know what they are doing—but we are never quite certain.

None of this widespread concern and interest is surprising. After all, the vast majority of us would prefer to survive.

"Diplomacy and defense are not substitutes for one another," as President Kennedy put it in one of his speeches. "At a time when a single clash could escalate overnight into a holocaust of mushroom clouds, a great power does not prove its firmness by leaving the task of exploring the other's intentions to sentries or those without full responsibility. Nor can ultimate weapons rightfully be employed, or the ultimate sacrifice rightfully demanded, until every reasonable solution has been explored."

This book is about the people whose job it is, in this nuclear age, to explore every reasonable solution. It explains the working of the diplomatic machinery for survival with which we are stuck, for better or for worse, and describes how the representatives of countries from the West, as well as from behind the Iron Curtain and the unaligned nations, tackle their job.

2:

The Origin
of the
Diplomatic Species

IN THE MIDDLE AGES, WHEN GOVERNMENT SERVICES HAD
to be staffed with ecclesiastics because they were the only
people who could read and write, some enthusiastic theolo-
gians advanced the claim that the first diplomats known to
mankind must have been the archangels, because they had
acted as messengers or "angeloi" between heaven and
earth.

It is a view of the origin of diplomacy that is not likely
to commend itself to Mr. Gromyko. Even the representatives of Christian nations like Mr. Dean Rusk and Lord
Home may find it vaguely embarrassing.

Nor can modern practitioners of the diplomatic art be

expected to approve of the god Hermes, whom the ancient Greeks regarded as the patron of ambassadors and heralds. For Hermes was also the protector of vagabonds, thieves and liars. On the morning he was born, he stole a herd of cattle from his brother Apollo, and then nipped back into his cradle to sleep soundly for the rest of the day. Zeus thought highly of his accomplishments and entrusted him with many delicate missions, but a modern selection board for the diplomatic service would not find him a very desirable candidate.

Diplomacy, unlike medicine, has no founding father figure, no Hippocrates. It just began when, in some dark, primordial forest of prehistoric days, two groups of savages, fighting over hunting boundaries, stolen cattle or abducted womenfolk, tired of slaughtering one another and became appalled at the prospect of mutual extermination.

Their difficulty, of course, was how to get their peace proposals to the other side. There is nothing more dangerous than to advance toward an enemy armed only with good intentions, and so those charged with what can be described as the earliest example of diplomatic activity surrounded themselves with an awe-inspiring air of superiority. They donned distinctive clothes, adorned their bodies with religious emblems to show they were sacrosanct, and assumed an immensely dignified demeanor to impress their fellows that they were different from other men. They had to be pompous to survive, and on the whole their methods were successful. It was a lesson that was not lost on subsequent generations of diplomats.

Every age has produced its own type of diplomat. First

there was the herald-diplomat, who was really little more than a glorified town crier. Wherever he was sent, he was received with elaborate ceremony and listened to in respectful silence, but his job was confined to delivering and taking messages. Discussion, argument and negotiation were no part of his duties, and a lively intelligence was not considered an advantage. All that was required of a herald was a sound constitution to withstand the rigors of travel through forests and across mountain ranges, a retentive memory and a loud voice.

The ancient Greek city-states were more demanding. Under their system, the diplomatic representatives of one city argued before the assembly of another. Instead of acting merely as messengers, they had to be advocates, skilled in conducting negotiations by public debate in the full glare of publicity. It was the most ambitious attempt in history to realize the ideal of open covenants openly arrived at. Certainly since then no one has tried to go as far.

The only trouble with the Greek system was that it did not work. Their diplomatic missions consisted of a number of ambassadors of equal standing, each representing a political faction in his city, and more of their time abroad was spent in keeping an eye on one another than in getting on with the job they had been sent to do. It was a favorite pastime to catch a political rival out in some indiscreet phrase and then, on returning home, to twist that chance remark into a charge of incompetence, corruption or even treason against him.

Small wonder, therefore, that the diplomats of those days soon developed the art of talking without saying anything. For they could not remain silent. They had to talk if they were not to run the risk of being accused of lack of zeal.

. Their speeches were noble monuments of classical oratory. They also included some of the most elaborate and long-winded exercises in ambiguous vacuity. For generations, they have been the despair of schoolboys wading through Thucydides. Even after a person has carefully translated each word, he is still left wondering what point there is to it all. The answer is very simple: those speeches were never meant to have a point.

The Romans had no time for such ingenious ineffectiveness. They liked things to be neat and tidy. They had treaties to cover practically every aspect of their relations with other countries, and if there is one thing that Rome did for diplomacy, it was to spread and strengthen the idea that treaties, like ordinary contracts, are, or ought to be, sacred.

Certainly Rome's record in observing and upholding treaties compares favorably with those of other nations, ancient and modern. Not that she can really claim very much credit for that. She made quite certain that the treaties she signed were so advantageous to her that there would have been no point in breaking them. She hardly ever bothered even to negotiate. In her view of the universe, there was Rome and then there was the rest—and the rest came nowhere.

Foreign ambassadors were handed the Roman draft of the treaty, and if there was too much argument, they were given a deadline. After that, they were stripped of their diplomatic privileges, proclaimed "spies" or "speculators" and escorted back to the frontier of their own country as prisoners. A Roman legion or two usually followed not long after.

It was a very one-sided form of diplomacy. Foreign ambassadors had the choice between acceptance or annihilation. Moreover, once a treaty had been accepted, the Romans saw to it that the other side did not feel tempted to ignore its obligations. They realized that it would be foolish, in view of all the circumstances leading up to the signature of the treaty, to rely exclusively on the other side's respect for the sanctity of treaties; and so they insisted on the surrender of hostages as a guarantee of good behavior.

The practice of delivering up diplomatic hostages did not commend itself to subsequent generations of statesmen, although there was an instance of it as late as 1748, when two British peers of the realm were surrendered to the French court as a guarantee for the return of Cape Breton to France. By all accounts they suffered no hardship. On the contrary, the tale of their adventures convinced their noble brethren in the Upper House that there was no better way of seeing Paris than as a hostage. The practice has since fallen into disuse.

If Rome was too strong to bother much about diplomacy, the Byzantine Empire was too weak to survive except by diplomacy. With scores of vigorous, bloodthirsty barbarian tribes on its borders, its only hope lay in playing off one potential enemy against another, and that called for accurate information about what went on in the minds of neighboring rulers.

The Byzantine Emperors met this problem by appointing more-or-less permanent ambassadors at foreign courts and asking them to send back regular reports to a department for external affairs in Constantinople. There all reports were carefully sifted, a policy was thrashed out, and instructions were drafted and dispatched, telling the ambassadors what line they should take.

It was the first time anyone had ever attempted to use diplomacy in a systematic, workmanlike, professional way, and visitors, especially from Western Europe, could not fail to be impressed with the advantages the system offered. The Venetians copied it from the Byzantines, and from Venice it spread to the Italian states, to Spain, France and the rest of the civilized world. Diplomacy became a recognized, essential part of statecraft which, it was realized, had to be organized with as much care and attention as a military campaign if it was to be effective.

The popularity of diplomats, however, did not keep step with their growing importance. For a long time most countries were loath to receive them. There was a feeling that they might learn too much, and no effort was spared to keep them from coming into contact with anyone who was not an official.

The Byzantine emperors graciously assigned foreign ambassadors luxurious quarters on their arrival. But once installed, the ambassadors found themselves virtually interned. Every time they tried to go out, an impressive-looking guard of honor came to attention, presented arms —and barred the way. And every time anyone who was not on official business called on them, he was told there was no one in.

At the same time, of course, the Byzantines wanted to impress foreign ambassadors with the might of their empire. For the benefit of the diplomatic corps, they mounted endless military parades, with the same troops entering by one gate, marching out by another, nipping round the back, changing uniforms and marching past again.

Above all, they went to a great deal of trouble to surround their emperor with an atmosphere of divine mystery. When an ambassador was led into the Imperial Presence, he had to prostrate himself on the floor, and on rising from the kowtow, he discovered that the emperor and his throne had risen up in the air as if by magic. What had happened was that a handful of slaves had lifted the throne by means of pulleys while everyone's forehead was touching the floor in deep and solemn obeisance. For further effect, the carved gilt lions at the side of the Chair of State belched forth fire and smoke and gave out most ominous roars.

It was all rather like a transformation scene in a pantomime, but let us not forget that pulleys and sham parades helped the Byzantine Empire to survive for over eleven centuries.

Other countries went to less trouble to mislead foreign ambassadors, but their methods of preventing diplomats from finding out what was really going on were frequently cruder. In Moscovy, up to the seventeenth century, foreign ambassadors who, in the opinion of the government, displayed too much curiosity, were simply thrown into jail. In Venice, citizens of the Republic were forbidden to have contact with foreign diplomats on pain of death. And Cromwell is reported to have threatened any member of Parliament who was caught talking to a foreign ambassador with immediate expulsion from the House of Commons.

Furthermore, even where kings and governments were ready to observe the proprieties of diplomatic intercourse, the street mob frequently was not. Good Queen Bess was always punctiliously courteous towards the envoys of His Most Catholic Majesty of Spain, but in the streets of London they could never be certain when they were liable to run into a shower of abuse and stones.

Fortunately, in our own enlightened times, ambassadors need no longer walk about in fear of their lives. The only survival of a rougher age is the so-called spontaneous students' demonstration. But that practice is confined to totalitarian states, and ambassadors have learned to take it in their stride.

A few years ago, in Madrid, hundreds of excited students were clamoring for the return of Gibraltar in front of the British embassy. Just as they seemed about to be breaking into the building, the telephone rang in the ambassador's study.

It was one of General Franco's Cabinet Ministers.

"Your Excellency," he said, "I am deeply distressed to learn what is happening outside your Embassy. How serious is the situation? Shall I send more police?"

"No, your Excellency," the ambassador replied, after thanking the minister for his solicitude, "please don't bother to send more police. Just send fewer students."

Suspicion and the risk of being manhandled by an angry mob were, however, not the only occupational hazards of a diplomat in the old days. There were many other inconveniences. Venetian ambassadors, for example, had to leave their families behind in Venice. They were not allowed to take their wives with them, "because wives are given to carrying tales and gossiping."

Then there was the problem of precedence. Until the Congress of Vienna decided, in 1815, that ambassadors should rank according to the date of their arrival, precedence depended on the seniority of their respective royal masters. Unfortunately, every monarch had his own ideas about his place in the royal scheme of things, and since no two crowned heads could ever agree, a diplomatic reception was rather like the last-minute rush for drinks in a public house when the landlord calls out, "Time, please," with everyone pushing, jostling and elbowing for position.

A diplomat's social life was undiluted misery. He could never relax and enjoy himself. He had to be ready to fight for his sovereign's pretensions at all times and by all means. At a Court Ball in London in 1768, the French envoy to his horror found the Russian ambassador sitting next to the ambassador of the Holy Roman Emperor in the front row of the diplomatic box. He knew his royal master, in his own estimation, ranked far above the Czar of all the Russias. He also knew that he could not expect the Russian to accept that view. And so he took the only course which in the circumstances seemed open to him as the solemnly accredited representative of His Most Christian Majesty of France. He climbed onto a chair in the back row of seats in the diplomatic box and jumped across into the front row so that he ended up between the two ambassadors. The Russian remonstrated in language that would have brought a blush to the cheek of a Billingsgate fishwife, and inevitably, as men of honor, the Russian and the Frenchman had to fight it out in a duel. The Russian was severely wounded.

There followed an exchange of vitriolic notes between the French and Russian Courts about the dignity and status of their respective crowns, but there is no record that either sovereign bothered to thank his representative for his trouble. Obviously the two diplomats did no more than was expected of them.

But by far the biggest headache of all diplomats was money. Kings and emperors, and even the great patrician republics, liked to be represented abroad with due pomp and circumstance, but paying for it was a different matter. There were, until fairly recently, no set scales of pay and allowance for diplomats on foreign assignments, and treasuries which in all countries at all times seem to have suffered from a chronic shortage of funds found it easy to turn a deaf ear to the desperate appeals for money from their representatives in far-off lands.

The Byzantine treasury at one time hit upon the ingenious idea of furnishing the Imperial ambassadors with goods and materials for sale abroad. It was soon discovered, however, that the ambassadors spent all their time in the market place making fabulous profits for themselves, and none on the business of His Byzantine Majesty. And so, with much regret, the practice had to be dropped.

Another ingenious idea that became popular in Europe at one stage was to save money on the frills and trimmings of diplomacy by picking artisans and servants as ambassadors instead of members of the ruling class. Louis XI of

France employed his barber in this way, and Florence a chemist, and by all accounts they did their job well.

No doubt the system of choosing men whose status made a retinue of servants and the provision of expensive lodgings unnecessary might have continued happily for a long time if some economy-minded states had not carried the whole thing too far. But a reaction set in when the diplomatic corps at a few of Europe's courts began to look like a collection of down-and-outs. The Pope was the first to object to the quality of the men sent to his court, and England's first Tudor king, Henry VII, who for years had to put up with a Spanish ambassador whose clothes crawled with lice and vermin, let it be known eventually that in the future he would not accept ambassadors who did not wash.

Very soon, states which had not been too proud to entrust their diplomatic business to traveling salesmen insisted that their interests abroad could be placed in the care of only their most blue-blooded aristocrats. Since blue blood and wealth went hand in hand in those days, it is not unreasonable to suppose that the motive behind this change was the same as that behind the employment of servants and artisans—to run diplomacy cheaply, at least as far as the state treasury was concerned. Certainly the new aristocratic ambassador was expected not only to pay for his journey, the upkeep of his residence abroad and any entertainment his job might entail, but also to provide out of his own pocket the salaries of any staff he needed in his embassy.

Naturally, this new dispensation was not very popular with the members of the high nobility. They did not mind

31

becoming army commanders, even if they had to pay the king's soldiers themselves, because they could usually recoup their outgoings and make a little on the side by sacking a town or two, but a diplomatic career offered no such compensations. On the contrary, it meant nothing but hardship. First, there was the prospect of long and uncomfortable days of travel over rough, unmade roads, and then one ran the risk of having to face insults from some uncouth foreign mob and from one's diplomatic colleagues—not to mention the possibility of ruining one's digestion eating strange, outlandish dishes. And to cap it all, one had to pay heavily for the privilege.

It seemed too much to ask of any man, and so it is not surprising, perhaps, that kings and governments sometimes resorted to methods not unlike those of the naval press gangs to induce their aristocracy to take up a diplomatic career. In Venice, a patrician who had been nominated for an ambassadorial post was not allowed to refuse, and if he was slow in taking up his appointment, he had to pay a heavy fine. The Florentine Republic at times conducted its reluctant ambassadors-designate to their posts under what was in theory a guard of honor and in practice an armed escort. And even the Sun King, Louis XIV, discovered, much to his chagrin, that frequently only threats could persuade the peers of his realm to accept the honor of representing him abroad.

To us, all this seems very strange. We cannot imagine a British ambassador to Washington being led reluctantly on to the "Queen Mary" at Southampton under a police escort to ensure that he will take up his post. Nor can we envisage an American ambassador-designate to the Court of St. James's being fined because he has shown himself dilatory in presenting himself to the Queen.

But then, of course, diplomacy, after an obscure beginning and many erratic and confused stages of development, has nowadays become not merely an important but a highly desirable profession. And diplomats, now that they have stopped jumping on one another, are considered quite a catch by most hostesses.

3:

How to
Become a
Diplomat

A BURNING DESIRE TO BRING THE DIFFERENT NATIONS and races of the world together is a laudable ambition, but those who do not feel that urge need not despair of becoming diplomats. It is not an essential requirement. Indeed, it can be a hindrance.

Like the judge who interrupted the soaring oratorical flight of a lawyer in his court with the remark, "Let's hear a little less about justice and a little more about the law," selection boards for the diplomatic service are inclined to distrust a flame that burns too pure. Love of humanity, in their view, is all very well, but in the meantime there is a job to be done. They regard diplomacy not as a vocation but as a profession demanding certain skills and aptitudes; and a candidate who appears too zealous to serve mankind in general is likely to be advised to forget diplomacy and to direct his energy into channels more suited to his talents, like the priesthood or politics.

Of course, no selection board ignores the personal appearance and bearing of a candidate. "He need not be an Apollo," Mr. Frank Aston-Gwatkin, a former Assistant Under Secretary at the British Foreign Office, once explained. "But he has to represent Great Britain; and the undersized, crablike, scruffy type simply will not do. These are not articles for export."

Britain has long enjoyed the reputation of being "good" at diplomacy, and her method of recruitment is regarded as a model in many parts of the world, though of course every country has its own way of doing things.

The United States Government sets about the task of recruiting its diplomats with all the verve and zest of a large business organization. Which it can hardly avoid doing unless it is prepared to sit back and see industry snap up all potential recruits in their last year at college. While the British Foreign Office becomes self-conscious and embarrassed when asked to define the type that is needed for the diplomatic service, the American State Department gives its answer with positive, punchy emphasis.

"The Foreign Service of the United States," it proclaims boldly, "is no place for dull, unimaginative persons. It calls for friendly, attractive personalities, sensitivity and intellectual curiosity, and a healthy sense of humor. If they are good at sport, so much the better. Natural brilliance is a great asset in the Service, but brilliance in itself is not enough; it is likely to burn itself out quickly unless it is accompanied by integrity, steadiness, sincerity and modesty."

Unexceptionable sentiments, but in the view of many old-time American professionals the type of examination to which a candidate has to submit at present does not test whether there is any brillance at all to burn itself out. As one of them put it, "The modern tests lack bite."

Until fairly recently a candidate faced papers in history, economics, law, mathematics and English that probed his knowledge, his capacity to marshal complex facts, and above all, his ability to express himself clearly and concisely, the most important prerequisite for success in diplomacy.

Following the recommendations of the Wriston Report in 1954, a new form of written examination was worked out by the Princeton Testing Service, and a candidate now contributes only a bare minimum of original writing. He has to put down his name and correct an English essay full of grammatical howlers and terminological inexactitudes. After that, his time is spent in putting X's against what he considers to be the answer to a series of multiple choice questions, even in his foreign language paper. With every question, he has a one-in-five chance of marking the right square whether he knows the correct answer or not.

He may, for example, have no idea whether the function of "settling accounts" of each of the administrative agencies of the United States Government is part of the work of the

    (A) Department of the Treasury
    (B) General Accounting Office

  (C) Bureau of the Budget
  (D) Head of each agency
  (E) Congress

But if, at a complete loss, he decides to go by word association and plump for the General Accounting Office, he will be right.

Again, his knowledge of veterans' legislation may be nil, and he may have no clue if faced with the question what advantage veterans have over non-veterans in Government jobs in respect to all of the following, except

  (A) appointment
  (B) reinstatement
  (C) retention
  (D) lay-off
  (E) pay

But if he has been around, he'll have learned that no government anywhere pays its servants a penny more than it has to, and go for (E)—and be correct.

Yet like all modern testing devices, these new examinations are trickier than they look. Four papers—English expressions, general ability, general background and modern language—are crammed into one day. The questions come fast and furious, and as in a hurdle race, once you lose pace and rhythm, you knock down first one hurdle and then another and finally fall flat on your face.

In most years more than eighty percent of candidates—the majority of them with at least college bachelor's degrees and many with M.A.'s and Ph.D's—have that unpleasant experience. The rest go forward to the next stage, the oral examination, which can last anything between one and two hours per candidate—more than enough time, in fact, to puncture any applicant's academic pretensions, expose the feebleness of his grasp of current problems, and reduce his command of English to incoherent mumblings.

It usually begins quite mildly and innocently. Why does the candidate want to join the Foreign Service? What does he regard as the most important United States achievement in the last ten years? Should Tito be treated as a friend or as an enemy?

After about a quarter of an hour the candidate may feel that he is coasting along nicely—until someone points out to him that he has contradicted himself twice. All at once the gentle probing appears to have become a ferocious inquisition. Relentlessly the panel members—Foreign Service professionals are always balanced by eminent businessmen, university professors and civic leaders—press on, and by the time the candidate is dismissed, he may well feel like a boned chicken.

"We don't mind if he doesn't know the answers; we frequently don't, either," a Foreign Service Officer with considerable experience on panels explains. "What matters is how a candidate behaves when he's at a loss."

In some years less than three percent of those who have survived the written examination to take the oral are passed—in other words, fewer than a hundred out of an original total of about four thousand candidates.

Even this drastically reduced but select band is not yet home and dry. It still faces two more hurdles, a physical examination and a loyalty investigation. While in Britain a candidate is merely reminded politely that he will not be appointed if his political views and affiliations should raise legitimate doubts about his reliability, in the United States he becomes the object of a full-scale "field security" check. His family, his friends, even mere acquaintances, are interviewed. With patient persistence, bit by bit, a complete picture of every facet of his life is built up: how he eats and sleeps, what he wears and reads, paints or writes, spends or lends, drinks and drives, twists and jives—until even the meekest mouse of an errant thought is cornered and caught. Only when the check is complete and positive can the candidate begin life as a freshman diplomat at the salary of $4,400 a year.

His opposite number in Britain starts at a lower salary, but he has passed through a test which not even the old professionals at the State Department who regret the disappearance of the pre-Wriston system in the United States would describe as lacking in academic bite. For the one qualification every aspirant to membership of the Senior Branch of the British Foreign Service must possess is a good university degree. He may have wealth, charm, family connections and polished manners, but without a first or second class honors degree—a mere pass degree is not enough—he will not even get as far as being allowed to take the mercilessly competitive entrance examination which leaves most candidates feeling like filleted fish. In some postwar years there have been as many as three hundred candidates for as few as twenty vacancies.

The examination is a grueling marathon affair, stretching over several weeks and divided into three stages. To begin with, there is a series of I.Q. tests which appear relatively simple and straightforward until candidates discover that their examination papers are generously peppered with deceptively innocent questions requiring remarkably subtle and complex answers. For example, they may be asked, "Does British political life suffer from a lack of idealism?" or, "What facts are the theories of psychologists intended to explain?" or, "Does universal suffrage promote political maturity?"

At the end of the first part, about half the candidates are eliminated. For those who survive, there next comes a treat known as the Weekend. It has nothing in common with the traditional English countryhouse weekend, except that it lasts for three days.

For a few years immediately after the war, it was actually held in a charming old Georgian manor house in Surrey, where, rumor had it, candidates were under constant observation, even during meals. The authorities tried their hardest to scotch that rumor, but without very much success. Some candidates remained convinced that even the number of times they brushed their teeth was duly noted somewhere, and others felt impelled to consume innumerable drinks at the bar in the evening in order to demonstrate their ability to stand up to the rigors of the diplomatic cocktail round. "The consequences of this entirely self-inflicted test," one of the Weekend examiners recalls wryly, "were at times unfortunate."

Today the Weekend is held in a less intoxicating, more mundane setting near London's fashionable tailors in Saville Row, where successful aspirants will later order their suits, and candidates are left to make their own arrangements about eating and sleeping—not because a humane government wants to spare aspiring diplomats unnecessary nervous wear and tear, but because the upkeep of the manor house proved rather expensive.

41

Despite the move, however, the Weekend remains a formidable obstacle race. Shortly after arrival, each candidate is handed a bulging file which contains a mass of data about some imaginary problem area. The area may be a mythical valley in the British Isles or some nonexistent island in the Indian Ocean, and the problems are certainly piled on thick. In the case of the island, candidates find that its population faces a balance of payments crisis, a housing shortage and the threat of partial unemployment, not to mention deep-seated racial and religious differences. All this is set out in the form of reports, letters and telegrams from an assortment of officials, just as it would be if this were not a mythical island.

Candidates are given a time limit in which to study the file and are then asked, again within a strictly limited period of time, to work out in writing a scheme for settling about a thousand refugees and their families from some other part of the world in the island.

The whole exercise is a devilishly clever test to see not only whether candidates can quickly absorb a confusing mass of facts and figures, penetrate to the heart of a problem and express their conclusions clearing and precisely, but also how, in our imperfect world, they face up to the delicate moral problem of striking a balance between principle and expediency.

The imaginary difficulties of the mythical problem area, which bear such a remarkable resemblance to the real difficulties of our day and age, continue to haunt the candidates throughout the Weekend. Formed into make-believe governmental committees, groups of candidates are asked to thrash out schemes for surmounting the housing or the employment problem, and under the watchful eyes of the ever-present examiners, each candidate takes his turn in the chair.

There are also group discussions in which candidates are encouraged to display their dialectic skill on ticklish subjects such as, "What should a career diplomat do if he is instructed to carry out a policy which he feels is wrong?" or, "Should a career diplomat stand by and see a friend get into trouble when he could drop a judicious hint, using some confidential information, and so save his friend?"

After this somewhat heavy fare, most candidates crave a change and turn almost with a sigh of relief to the series of searching interviews which are part and parcel of the Weekend. But relief is short-lived and candidates soon discover that the interviews are no joke. There are, in fact, three of them, one with each of three examiners, and one of the examiners is always a psychologist.

As a rule, the interviews begin in a deceptively gentle atmosphere of sweet reasonableness. "Where would you travel," one examiner, for example, may ask with a kindly, avuncular smile, "given, say, three hundred pounds and a free month or two?"

If the candidate replies, "The United States," the next question, put in the same smooth, unhurried tone, is likely to be, "What, then, do you think are the main problems at issue between the United States and Britain at the moment?" And before the interview is five minutes old, the hapless candidate finds himself inextricably committed to explaining why the rich cream of Anglo-American relations occasionally turns sour.

Another examiner may open the bowling by asking the

candidate to write down any proposition that he is prepared to defend. It does not matter whether the proposition reads, "Monogamous marriage is one of the cornerstones of Western civilization," "Communism is evil" or "The earth is round." The examiner will take a view that is diametrically opposed. He will attack the candidate's case and twist his every argument. He will needle him into losing his temper and charm him into letting down his guard, until after forty minutes or so the candidate neither knows nor cares what it was he set out to defend. Indeed, by the time he is dismissed, the candidate probably feels certain that the only comment the examiner can make on his performance is, "Unable to stick to his guns under pressure."

In its final trials, however, the Weekend employs not a club but a rapier on its victims. On the last day the candidates are asked to write two character sketches of themselves, one as though drawn by a "discerning critic," the other as by an "appreciative friend." And just before leaving, every candidate has to grade his fellow competitors in order of preference (a) as potential diplomats and (b) as holiday companions.

The Weekend, like the series of I.Q. tests, is a great eliminator. Only about half of those who went in for it enter the third and last stage of the entrance examination —an interview before the Final Selection Board, a formidable body consisting of the Chairman of the Civil Service Commission, a university professor, an ex-ambassador, the Head of the Foreign Office Personnel Department, a woman leader, a business executive, and possibly a trade union leader. They are the ultimate judges.

As a candidate is ushered into their presence, he notices, spread out before each of them, a dossier which records in an impersonal, distilled form all his successes and failures almost from the day he was born—his school and university career, his army service, if any, and all his sins and omissions during the previous stages of the examination.

It can be an unnerving experience, and many candidates, after all they have been through, are at a loss to find a satisfactory answer to even so simple a question as "Why do you want to become a diplomat?" What had once seemed such an ordinary ambition suddenly appears to be a prize beyond the reach of the average mortal.

And so, of course, it is. Depending on the number of vacancies, only one in four or five or even six out of those who are interviewed by the Final Board can hope to make the grade.

But for the candidate who successfully clears this last hurdle, the future is bright. He joins one of the most select fraternities in the world, the Senior Branch of the Foreign Office, which, including ambassadors and the Permanent Under Secretary of State, numbers only just over seven hundred. No matter how junior he may feel, he is not expected to "sir" his superiors. His colleagues will gladly put him up for their club, usually either the Travellers' or the St. James's, and although his starting salary as a Third Secretary on probation may only be a third of that of his opposite number in the United States—as both climb the ladder of promotion, the gap in salary scales narrows noticeably—there beckons in the distance the prospect of one day being dubbed a knight and addressed as "Your Excellency."

The casual observer may easily jump to the conclusion that competitive entrance examinations have done little to dispel the aura of aristocratic privilege that has always tended to enshroud the Foreign Office, but facts and figures prove otherwise. Admittedly eighty-five percent of all new entrants still come from Oxford and Cambridge, but that is not a fair guide, because the two ancient universities today attract all the best students in the country, no matter what their schools may have been. Looking at schools alone, the proportion of public school entrants has since 1938 dropped from eighty-five percent to about forty-five percent. Her Britannic Majesty's ambassadors today include, or are about to include, sons of miners, dockers, taxi drivers and bus conductors. And such is the tradition of the Service that even the shrewdest observer is incapable of telling the difference between them and the scions of the nobility. As in America, where the Foreign Service is often accused of being the exclusive preserve of well-heeled Harvard, Yale and Princeton graduates (in fact less than twenty-five percent took their bachelor degrees there, and many of those went on scholarships), the profession of diplomacy quickly rubs away differences of background, education and social position. It would be a bold sociologist who claimed that he could walk into an American or British embassy these days, and simply by observing the diplomatic staff at work and play, spot each man's home state or country, school, college and family background. If a betting man, he would lose a lot of money.

Undoubtedly the country that makes it most difficult to become a diplomat is France. In a murderous mixture of lengthy oral and written tests, candidates have to pit their knowledge against the examining skill of an array of professors on subjects such as English and German, history, geography, international law and philosophy. They also have to show that they are intimately acquainted with most of French literature and all that is best in foreign writing. Moreover, their prose must have style and distinction. The French diplomatic service has included many brilliant authors, and senior officials at the Quai d'Orsay are not prepared to put up with lack of grace and style in the reports of their colleagues from abroad as well as with a perpetually grim international situation.

Of course, French diplomatic standards had to be exceptionally high under the Third and Fourth Republics because French diplomats frequently had to shoulder far heavier responsibilities than any of their foreign colleagues. In British constitutional theory, the acts of every diplomat are the acts of the Foreign Secretary. It is he who lays down foreign policy, and it is he who is responsible to Parliament.

French constitutional theory, broadly speaking, was much the same. The trouble in practice was that there was frequently no Foreign Minister. Under General de Gaulle the position has changed considerably. It is the President who lays down policy, and what the Foreign Minister has gained in security of tenure he has lost in independence of action. He is little more than the President's principal diplomatic agent.

The West German entrance examination is less exacting, but new entrants are kept on probation for longer than anywhere else and have to pass a series of tests at prescribed intervals—no doubt on the bureaucratically rational principle that since diplomacy involves many aspects of knowledge and activity, there is no point in confirming a man in his job until he is duly and properly qualified and certificated in every one of them.

Of course Germany's troubles in recruiting diplomats after the war were considerably more complicated than those of other countries. She had to find not only Third Secretaries, but also ambassadors, because many of her senior diplomats were tainted by the Hitler regime.

One method adopted by the Foreign Ministry in Bonn was to fill the yawning gaps in the upper echelons of its diplomatic service from the ranks of Germany's princely houses. But even that was liable to lead to complications.

When Dr. Adenauer some years ago offered an ambassadorship to a prince of the former Bavarian Royal House, the Wittelsbachs, he was told that the prince could not accept without the consent of the Head of his House, the former Crown Prince Rupprecht of Bavaria. The Head of the Wittelsbachs was approached formally and in due course informed the German Chancellor that he was graciously pleased to give his consent, "provided acceptance was not construed to imply that the Royal House of Bavaria recognized, consented to or agreed to abide by the recent political changes in Germany."

There was considerable consternation in Bonn. Were the Wittlesbachs challenging the legitimacy of the newborn Federal Republic? Dr. Adenauer's staff made discreet inquiries and discovered, much to their relief, that Crown Prince Rupprecht, who was then in his eighties, was referring not to the events following 1945, but to the happenings—several Reichs ago—in 1918, when his father, Ludwig III, had been forced to vacate the Bavarian throne.

Naturally, in this age of intense diplomatic activity, foreign offices are constantly seeking to improve their methods of choosing diplomats. The most ominous portent of what we must expect comes from Washington, where the State Department has now officially recognized the importance of diplomats' wives.

"We may be behind industry in thinking about wives," a spokesman explained, "but we are coming round to the view that a man's wife may make him or break him in some posts."

Never slow in following up its policy conclusions with action, the State Department has started a school where wives, before going off abroad for the first time with their freshman diplomat husbands, may take courses not only in diplomatic etiquette—to help them solve teasers like placing in the right order Britain's Lord Privy Seal, an archbishop, a deposed king, the Chief Justice of the United States Supreme Court, and the foreign ministers of Belgium, Rumania and Nigeria—but also in policy, economics and languages.

It may seem a useful idea, and no doubt many other countries will eventually take it up. But where is it going to end? What happens if the wife fails to make the grade? Does the husband choose another career or another wife?

4:

Short Cuts to Becoming a Diplomat

CAREER DIPLOMATS ARE A CLANNISH LOT WHO DO NOT like non-union labor in their profession. For an outsider who has not gone through the mill the prospects in most countries of becoming an ambassador are not very bright. In Britain he stands no chance at all, except in times of crisis, when Prime Ministers and Foreign Secretaries have been known to insist that international affairs are too serious a matter to be left to mere professionals.

When that happens, the career men are liable to find the "plum" posts in the Service rudely snatched from their grasp. On the outbreak of war in 1939, the Washington embassy was promptly handed over to Lord Lothian, a distinguished Liberal politician and administrator. Later on, in 1940, Churchill prevailed on Lord Halifax to step down from the Foreign Secretaryship to go to the United States, just as he persuaded Sir Stafford Cripps to take over the British embassy in Moscow. The moment Paris was liberated in 1944, the embassy there went not to a career man but to Duff Cooper, a former Tory Cabinet Minister who had resigned from the Chamberlain government in protest against Munich. In 1948, when Britain and Europe ran into serious economic difficulties, Bevin, who then presided at the Foreign Office, sent to Washington Sir Oliver Franks, a university professor who, he felt, knew more about the problems of the day than all the professionals put together. And in 1961 Mr. Macmillan persuaded Sir David Ormsby-Gore, a personal friend of the Kennedy clan since prewar days, to resign his seat in the House of Commons and his post as Minister of State at the Foreign Office, to take charge of the Washington embassy. In most cases, however, the professionals have eventually been successful in winning back their embassies.

In Germany, the outsider's chances are almost equally slender. Admittedly the postwar shortage of senior career men free of the taint of Naziism gave a temporary opening to a few "amateurs," but now that a new generation of professionals is coming along, the tidy Teutonic mind once again frowns on the employment of the nonexpert who has not had the benefit of a thorough professional training. In a few cases, however, fulsome devotion to the cause of Dr. Adenauer and his Christian Democrats has been accepted as an adequate substitute.

In France, too, the path of the outsider is difficult; and

if his heart is set on wresting an ambassadorship, even one of the lesser ones, from the professionals, he will have to resort to tactics that are, to say the least, tortuous. In the first place, he must somehow contrive to become a key figure in the internal administration of the country, such as the prefect of a department. Secondly, he must make an effort to fall foul of the politicians in Paris. For French politicians do not like being crossed on their home ground, and if they are, tend to retaliate by treating diplomacy as an occasional dumping ground for public nuisances.

As for the Soviet Union, a smooth, impersonal, almost faceless professional uniformity is the order of the day. Among the blandly efficient diplomatic technicians of the Zorin-Zarubin-Malik-Gromyko vintage, one is not likely to discover even the smallest personal idiosyncrasy, not even a goatee beard such as Mr. Maisky, the wartime ambassador in London, used to sport.

Of course there was a time when the Bolsheviks were less hidebound and took a mischievous delight in cocking a snook at so-called bourgeois, capitalistic conventions. In the early nineteen-twenties Lenin appointed someone who was not only an outsider but a woman—the colorful Alexandra Kollontai—to be the first madam Ambassador in history, and so unwittingly blazed a trail for Mrs. Perle Mesta, Mrs. Clare Boothe Luce and Mrs. Pandit.

Diplomats throughout the world were deeply shocked. Apart from belonging to the wrong sex, Madame Kollontai had a past record suggesting a strong trait of eccentricity. An aristocrat by birth, she had been a member of Lenin's first Politburo; had married one of the heroes of the Revolution, a sailor who had helped to conquer Petrograd for the Bolsheviks; and as People's Commissar for Social Welfare had advocated the advantages of trial marriages.

Before long, however, the diplomats of other nations learned to respect Madame Kollontai's abiliity and shrewdness. In comparison with the run-of-the-mill representatives of the Soviet Union, she was gay, witty and entertaining. Stalin once called her "our Madame de Stael," and an American diplomat who served in Stockholm at the same time she did admitted, "She may have been a Red, but she certainly was what the French call 'une grande dame.'"

Nowadays the Soviet diplomatic service as a rule does not employ outsiders, however gifted they may be; and if an exception is made, the outsider knows that as far as the Party is concerned he has become the odd man out. In the late nineteen-twenties Kamenev, who had opposed Stalin, was neatly isolated from his friends in Moscow by being despatched to the Soviet embassy in Rome. Nine years later, Stalin took more direct action to eliminate Kamenev's influence. He had him accused of treason and executed. More recently Krushchev decided that the best way of banishing Molotov from politics was to appoint him ambassador in Outer Mongolia's capital, Ulan Bator, which very few of even the most assiduous students of international affairs had ever heard of and certainly none had regarded as a hive of diplomatic activity.

In fact, there remains only one country in the world where an amateur, irrespective of whether he is an engineer, a businessman, a banker, an insurance broker, a lawyer or a university professor, can still become an ambassador without bothering about examinations or qualifications of any sort—the United States. There is only one proviso: he must be a millionnaire.

The procedure is perfectly straightforward. Some time before a Presidential election he simply spreads the word among his friends in either the Democratic or the Republican Party—depending on his political sympathies—that he is interested in serving the cause of the United States in some capacity abroad, and eventually one of his party's money gatherers will call on him and suggest that he make a contribution to campaign funds.

If the Presidential candidate he has supported is successful in the subsequent elections, he will in due course get his reward—an ambassadorship and the privilege of meeting most of the expenses of his appointment out of his own pocket. Always providing of course, that he coughed up enough in the way of a campaign contribution. During the 1956 campaign some of the Republican fund raisers hinted as delicately as they could that in an era of rising prices and inflationary spirals contributors with diplomatic ambitions would have to give deep bronchial coughs if they did not want to be disappointed, and it is no secret that one hopeful aspirant whose cough only reached the sum of $7,000 was passed over.

Naturally, the party that loses usually condemns this practice in ringing tones of outraged self-righteousness and accuses the winners of jeopardizing American's foreign policy by crudely placing responsible diplomatic posts on the auction block and selling them for cash on the barrelhead.

But this sort of charge should be dismissed as a case of sour grapes. In any event, only about a third of all American ambassadorships are still distributed under this system of political patronage. The rest are now held by professionals, largely, it must be admitted, because appointments behind the Iron Curtain and in the obscurer parts of Africa and Asia do not carry a great deal of social prestige in the eyes of the amateur and his wife and are therefore not very much sought after. And where important posts like London and Paris are involved, the qualifications and suitability of the would-be ambassador are as carefully investigated as his bank balance. Certainly no one has come forward to suggest that the American amateur ambassadors in London or Paris over the last twenty or thirty years have been less effective and successful at their jobs than their British or French professional counterparts in Washington.

It would be wrong, however, to suppose that entry by checkbook presents no hazards. According to the American Constitution, every ambassadorial nomination must be approved by the Senate before it becomes effective, and by the time an ambassador designate has been put through his paces by the Senate's Foreign Relations Committee, which has the power to veto all nominations, he may well feel that the examinations and interviews for the professional diplomatic service cannot be much worse.

In 1957, Mr. Gluck, the head of a flourishing system of chain stores, was nominated ambassador to Ceylon, and the following dialogue took place between him and Senator Fulbright of Arkansas.

SENATOR FULBRIGHT:

How much did you contribute to the Republican Party in the 1956 election?

MR. GLUCK:

Well, I wouldn't know offhand, but I made a contribution.

SENATOR FULBRIGHT:

Well, how much?

MR GLUCK:

Let's see . . . I would say in all twenty or thirty thousand dollars.

SENATOR FULBRIGHT:

If you contributed thirty thousand dollars, don't you think Ceylon is rather a remote post for that? The one who went to Belgium only contributed eleven thousand dollars.

MR. GLUCK:

I don't think I want to admit that is the principal reason.

SENATOR FULBRIGHT:

What do you think is the principal reason?

MR. GLUCK:

Well, my interest to find something in Government life that I would like to do.

SENATOR FULBRIGHT:

What are the problems in Ceylon you think you can deal with?

MR. GLUCK:

One of the problems are the people there. I believe I can —I think I can establish unless we—again, unless I run into something that I have not run into before—a good relationship and good feeling towards the United States.

SENATOR FULBRIGHT:
Do you know who the Prime Minister of India is?

MR. GLUCK:
Yes, but I can't remember his name.

SENATOR FULBRIGHT:
Do you know who the Prime Minister of Ceylon is?

MR. GLUCK:
His name is a bit unfamiliar now. I cannot call it off.

The Senate in due course approved Mr. Gluck's nomination. Mr. Dulles, the Secretary of State, went on record as saying that he, too, would find it difficult to recall the names of all the statesmen with whom he had to deal unless he were carefully briefed beforehand. And so another blow was struck for the cause of the amateur in diplomacy.

It only remains to be added that when the then Prime Minister of Ceylon, Mr. Bandaranaike, heard of the incident, he dismissed the whole business by saying that he was not in the least surprised; in his four years at Oxford University he had found only two people who could pronounce and write his name correctly. He and Mr. Gluck got on extremely well together, and the American was a great success as ambassador!

Indeed, amateurs often are, especially when they are friends of close associates of the President and can take the liberty of cutting through the hierarchical chain of command and getting on directly to the White House—as Mr. J. K. Galbraith, the United States ambassador to

India, did to some effect in 1962 when the Chinese Communists invaded the North East Indian border region.

Understandably this procedure is not popular with the professionals. It merely confirms their suspicion of short cuts of every kind.

5:

America's
Diplomacy
in Action

MANY AMERICANS REGARD DIPLOMACY AS VIRTUALLY AN "un-American activity," invented by foreigners for the benefit of foreigners. America, they claim, has never lost a war and never won a conference. They argue in tones of dismay edged with satisfaction (because their thesis somehow to them seems to prove America's moral superiority) that her diplomats are constantly outthought, outmaneuvered, trounced and trampled on in every encounter across a green baize table with the cunning, calculating, double-crossing representatives of other powers.

This is a curiously distorted view of American diplomacy—the more so since it bears no relation to the facts.

Few countries in the world have reaped as rich dividends from the skillful use of diplomacy as the United States. Indeed, there would probably be no United States today but for the efforts of her diplomats.

At the tenderest, most vulnerable stage of her development Benjamin Franklin won the support of powerful France. Holland was persuaded a little later on to pump much-needed economic aid into the infant Republic. Thomas Jefferson's and James Monroe's purchase of Louisiana in 1803 and William Seward's acquisition of Alaska in 1867 at a cost of about a penny an acre eliminated France and Russia from the North American Continent. And during the Civil War America's representatives delicately but firmly headed off the danger of British and French intervention.

In none of these episodes could the United States be said, by any stretch of the imagination, to have negotiated from strength. Patience, persistence and persuasion, with a generous dash of guile and gamesmanship in playing off the great European powers one against the other, were her only weapons. And throughout those early years her diplomatic corps consisted of a tiny handful of men operating on a shoestring.

When Thomas Jefferson became Secretary of State in 1790, the State Department had a staff of four clerks and one French translator. The sum total voted by Congress for all representation abroad was $40,000, equivalent to about two ambassadorial salaries in minor capitals today. United States consuls received no payment at all. They were expected to make do on the fees they collected on trade and personal documents they had to issue in the course of their duties—and in large trading centres like London, Antwerp, Hamburg and Genoa they did very well. The public purse strings were held so tight that even at the beginning of this century the nation owned only four embassies and legations; and two of those, at Seoul and Bangkok, were presents from the kings of Korea and Siam because they felt sorry for America's accredited representatives. Everywhere else, United States diplomats were left to make their own arrangements for working and living quarters.

Foreign policy was simple in those days, of course, and its objectives were easily pinpointed: to keep the United States out of entangling alliances and other powers out of the Americas, so as to give the country time to grow and gather strength. It needed no policy planners or brain trusters to spell out the obvious. America's diplomats knew what they had to do, and Congress was content to let them get on with the job, provided it cost next to nothing —or, if possible, less. Even presidential pronouncements on foreign policy were few and far between. President Wilson's inaugural address in 1913 contained not one single word on foreign affairs.

Today, not only is the United States entangled in alliances but Washington is the very center of the most extensive network of international commitments ever devised. After more than a century and a half of studied aloofness, it suddenly finds itself captain and team manager of one of the two main power blocs in the world. Small wonder, therefore, that after the Second World War the State Department literally burst out of its old and architecturally somewhat overornate home next to the White House and

63

had to be accommodated in a vast, gleaming, new edifice a little way east of the Potomac river in a spot bearing the rather unfortunate name of "Foggy Bottom."

Entering "State's" new home, the visitor looks in vain for the shabby Victorian leisureliness of London's Foreign Office or the eighteenth-century, stylized ornateness of Paris's Quai d'Orsay. The bright corridors sparkle and shine with antiseptic cleanliness. J. K. Galbraith, President Kennedy's ambassador to India, once called the place "the ice palace." The elevators there move as smoothly and swiftly as in any mammoth corporation's modern headquarters. In the Foreign Office they are decidedly sluggish; in the Quai d'Orsay, noticeably creaky. The office furniture in Washington is strictly mid-twentieth-century functional. London clings to the last century and Paris to the century before that.

It is very different from other foreign ministries, most of which still prefer homes that do not resemble modern business blocks too closely. But once a visitor puts a query on a specific foreign policy problem, he is likely to discover that the latest in steel filing cabinets, a highly efficient interoffice communications system, and a galaxy of extraordinarily competent as well as attractive secretaries do not always produce an answer more rapidly than anywhere else. On the contrary, it often takes a good deal longer. For, as any State Department official will explain with just a touch of sadness, " 'State' is no longer alone in the foreign policy field. The Pentagon, with its overseas bases; the Treasury; Commerce; the Central Intelligence Agency—even the Department of Agriculture, with its vast food surpluses—all want to have their say. In fact if you're unlucky, you can have more than three dozen Government departments and agencies trying to get into the act." The result is sometimes a seemingly endless round of consultations, checks and clearances.

In theory, of course, the process by which United States foreign policy is formulated and executed looks simple and straightforward. Policies are initiated by the President. His principal advisor and executive arm is the Secretary of State, aided and supported by the State Department. The Senate has the right to veto all senior appointments from the Secretary of State downward, and to ratify or reject treaties, and both houses of Congress have to give their approval if a policy needs fresh legislation or—as it almost invariably does these days—dollars.

In practice however, these simple ground rules give the outsider no inkling of the complexity of the game. For that, he would have to attend the Secretary of State's daily staff meeting, which can be called for as early as 8 A.M. and rarely meets later than 9:30 A.M., depending on the routine the Secretary of State likes to follow. Washington's daily diplomatic round swings into top gear at least one or two hours earlier in the morning than that of most of the world's other capitals.

Let us suppose, then, that the visitor is allowed to join "State's" top brass—the No. 2, the Under Secretary; the No. 3, the Under Secretary for political affairs, one of whose chief functions is liaison with the Pentagon; their two Deputy Under Secretaries; the Counselor who is not a legal expert but a brains truster, an ideas man in charge of policy planning; and the eleven Assistant Secretaries, five of whom are in charge of the regional bureaus—

Europe, Inter-American Affairs, Africa, the Near East and South Asia, and the Far East—and six of whom deal with such subjects as economic affairs, relations with Congress, international organizations, and education and culture.

The meeting usually opens with a brief report by the Director of the Bureau of Intelligence and Research on important developments and trends throughout the world within the last twenty-four hours. The Secretary of State may add a comment or two of his own before asking if anyone has any problems he cannot settle at his level.

At this point the Assistant Secretary for the Near East and South Asia may mention that a message has reached him from the United States embassy in a certain Asian country, through that country's "desk" in his regional bureau, that the Asian government in question is about to ask for American aid. The government is neutralist, at times indeed decidedly pro-Communist, but this seems a good chance to try to pry it out of the tightening Communist grip. Moreover, such a gesture may well have a similar effect on its neutralist neighbors.

The Assistant Secretary for Economic Affairs supports the granting of aid. His staff, he explains, has just completed a study of the country's economy, and aid injected at the right points could quickly produce striking results for all to see.

The Assistant Secretary for Europe is less enthusiastic. The country has recently expropriated the property of most of the British and French living there in a most ruthless manner. Relations between it and Britain and France are pretty strained at the moment, and America's two

European allies would be bound to regard American aid at this stage as a calculated slap in the face and would hardly be very receptive to any suggestions about the need for closer cooperation which the Secretary of State may wish to bring up at the NATO meeting in Paris in two months' time.

The Assistant Secretary for International Organizations likes the aid idea because it is bound to win the United States friends among the uncommitted nations at the United Nations, but the Assistant Secretary for Congressional Relations asks if the project could not be shelved for a while. A certain senator, he points out, is facing a very tough fight for re-election and is desperately looking around for an issue to whip up a little enthusiasm for his campaign: opposition to this aid project might be it, and since he happens to be the chairman of a key committee, he could, if re-elected on a no-aid-for-neutralists or crypto-Communists ticket, prove a very awkward customer on all aid questions in future.

The Assistant Secretary for the Near East and South Asia intervenes to say that aid in this case would have to be given quickly and generously if it is to have the desired political effect in his region, and the Assistant Secretary for Public Affairs states that the reasons for helping neutralist nations are being increasingly understood by the American public and that he would anticipate nothing very serious in the way of American press opposition if the scheme went ahead.

The Secretary of State says that although he is basically in favor, the question would need further study. He asks the Assistant Secretary for Congressional Relations to sound out opinion on the Hill, the Assistant Secretary for Europe to discover if Britain and France are contemplating any further moves in the near future to secure compensation for their citizens in the Asian country, and the Assistant Secretary for the Near East and South Asia to explore what pressure the United States can bring on the Asian country "behind the scenes" to induce it, without loss of face, to settle its difference with Britain and France. Everyone is to report back to a special ad hoc committee which is to work out an agreed recommendation to be presented to the President as soon as the Asian country's request is formally received.

High-level, streamlined ad hoc committees are, in fact, Washington's prescription for speedy action on urgent problems. But even these have to be watched. For Washington's administrative jungle is not unlike the tropical forests of Borneo: both have a habit of reclaiming quickly any clearing that may have been hacked out of their luxuriant undergrowth. When President Kennedy set up a "Berlin Task Force" to keep an eye on the crisis there, it started life as a small interdepartmental committee of a dozen men. Some months later so many bureaus and agencies had won the right to be represented on it that its membership had risen to sixty.

Less-than-urgent problems are denied the ad hoc committee short cut. They have to take their place in the pipeline; and since every query involves more than one office at the Washington end—even if it is only a request by an ambassador abroad somewhere to have the ceiling of his bedroom repainted—replies can be a long time a-coming.

Some United States embassies try to jump the queue by giving their communications a spurious air of urgency. They send telegrams when a letter would do, or mark some routine missives "priority" or "NIACT," that is to say, requiring immediate attention at any time of the night or day.

Most State Department hands are up to these tricks. A young Second Secretary at a United States embassy in the Near East who was exceptionally persistent in his badgering for an answer to his particular request was reminded that he was due to begin a tour of duty at "State" in six months—"just in time to draft a reply himself."

The two-way flow of telegrams and despatches in and out of the Department is such that its communications center handles more than half a million words on an average day. Apart from those, the desks of the people working at "State" are frequently awash with information papers, notes, reports, requests and memoranda from Defense, Interior, the United States Information Agency, Justice, foreign embassies in Washington, congressmen and church leaders, to mention just a few.

At times, in fact, the whole establishment is like a tiny ship battered by mountainous waves of paper, and men— and problems—are apt to be temporarily submerged. In 1945 no less a matter than a Soviet request for an American loan of one billion dollars disappeared somewhere in the fastnesses of the Department's files for six months. The Russians, of course, thought that the "loss" was "diplomatic," and old hands at "State" still recall how they failed to convince them that the explanation was muddle and not Machiavelli.

None of the columnists and commentators who regularly flay the State Department for being paper-logged has yet come up with a solution to its difficulties—probably because there is none. After all, the United States Government can act effectively only if its many branches are kept in step; alliances that stretch across the five continents of the globe can work together only if they think together; and all this requires information, consultation and discussion. Which brings us back to where we started. The circle is complete—and vicious.

The men at the center and the perimeter of that circle, who provide the professional diplomatic hard core among "State's" fifteen thousand employees, are the Foreign Service officers, roughly four thousand in number, of whom between one thousand two hundred and one thousand five hundred are usually on duty in the States while the rest man the three hundred outposts, ranging from enormous embassies to minuscule consulates, which the United States maintains abroad. They have survived the competitive entrance examination into the Service which dates back to only 1924, the initial "in-service" orientation course and their first two-year stint of duty at "State" to begin the slow ascent up the promotion ladder from vice-consul or Third Secretary. Their early years are spent stamping visas, drafting letters, reports and speeches for their seniors, bailing United States citizens out of foreign jails and seeing that a car is always there at the appointed hour and place to meet the ambassador's wife after her shopping expeditions.

But with seniority comes more responsibility, a bigger desk, a grander office, a growing assortment of mementos from foreign assignments—Austrian meerschaums, African blowpipes and Indian ivory—and the faculty of ceasing to be surprised at man's foibles. They have learned that politicians, their own included, play politics; that every new President wants to revamp the United States Foreign Service and eventually settles for what he has got, especially once he has won his second term; that while American aid is always acceptable, American advice is much less so; that nations that practice cannibalism have no difficulty in subscribing to the high principles of the United Nations; that while, in Churchill's phrase, it is better "to jaw-jaw than to war-war," silence is sometimes golden; and that their political chiefs will not always stand up for them against the investigating fury of a Congressional committee. In short, they know the score.

For many a European diplomat the position of his American colleagues is a constant source of amazement and pain. Brought up in the tradition that a foreign ministry is the preserve of professionals in which changing political chiefs are quickly taught the art of bowing gracefully to the superior knowledge of their permanent experts, he is appalled that every incoming President should be able to alter the whole of the State Department's top echelon, right down to Assistant Secretary level. His sense of hierarchical propriety is outraged by the fact that the professionals have no recognized spokesman, no Secretary-General, no Permanent Under Secretary of State. And while his face may light up when he is told that President Eisenhower once promoted a career man, Robert Murphy, to the No. 2 job in the State Department, his gloom is bound to return as soon as he learns that the occupants of all top jobs in "State," whether they be career or non-career men, are tenants at will—the President's will.

A French diplomat once dismissed the system as "tent camp diplomacy" adding, "How can there be continuity of policy without security of tenure for the professional?" The problem troubles few American Foreign Service officers. Being practical men, they know that the American political system is not likely to be turned upside down and inside out to bring it into line with European practice. In any case, the system ensures continuity in its own way, for successes among the outsiders are apt to be called back time and again. Over the last twenty years or so, and under three Presidents, amateur Averell Harriman has held more top jobs in and around the State Department than any career man. The late John Foster Dulles learned the ways of "State" as a special negotiator and as United States representative at the United Nations long before he became President Eisenhower's Secretary of State; and when President Kennedy, at the height of the Cuban crisis in October, 1962, had to despatch someone to explain his moves to Europe's leaders, he chose "amateur" Dean Acheson.

What divides the professionals from the "amateurs" is generally not expertise but the right to a pension. Both know the form and, as a rule, one another. When Dean Rusk's appointment as Secretary of State was first announced, most diplomats in Europe hurriedly reached for their reference books to discover who the new man was. There was no such anxious flurry of checking at "State." There they knew their man.

He had served with them first as Head of the Office of

Special Political Affairs, then as deputy Under Secretary; and when "State's" Far Eastern Division came under heavy fire following the collapse of the Chiang Kai Chek forces on the Chinese mainland, he had voluntarily stepped down to become Far Eastern Assistant Secretary to rebuild morale and organization in the Division.

It was he who had introduced a "round-the-clock watch" at the State Department, as a result of which there is now always one of the eleven Assistant Secretaries on duty; and as luck would have it, Rusk was the duty officer on the night of June 25, 1950, when the United States ambassador in Seoul cabled the news that Communist troops had invaded South Korea. Sensing that the temporary Soviet boycott of the United Nations Security Council gave the United States and the United Nations a unique opportunity for action, he had telephoned the Secretary of State, Dean Acheson, in the middle of the night to ask for permission to contact Trygvie Lie, then United Nations Secretary-General, with the request to summon the Security Council in emergency session and so launched the political and military strategy which was to stop the Communists. A noncareer man—one of the many who move in and out of top diplomatic posts—he had left the Government service two years later, not to return until summoned by President Kennedy to take over the No. 1 post at "State" in 1961. The reaction among the professionals was that he would be able to pick up the threads of his job in a day, "as if he were walking from one office into another."

Nor does the average Foreign Service officer appear to experience any deep sense of frustration when European diplomats complain that under the American system he can never hope to become ambassador at a "plush" embassy like London, Paris or Rome. His reply, as likely as not, will be that he is jolly glad he can't, since he would have to supply the "plush" out of his own pocket, to the tune of about $100,000 a year in the case of London, where the official entertainment allowance for the ambassador is a mere $8,000, or to the tune of $60,000 a year in Rome, where it is $6,000.

The position is not much better in some of the smaller European countries. In Austria it comes to a meager $4,000, and in Ireland to no more than $2,500—which is not even enough to pay for the one annual entertainment no United States ambassador dares fail to provide, the Fourth of July party.

Career men console themselves with the thought that millionaires and their wives are less keen on the social round behind the Iron Curtain or in the hot, steamy capitals of emerging Africa. "They are quite willing to leave these spots to us," they explain laconically.

What does rile them, however, is Congressional meanness on allowances for junior United States diplomats. The sum total, for all United States representational entertainment abroad in 1962, was less than one million dollars and barely $100,000 more than in 1961, although the United States had in the meantime had to open fourteen new embassies and three consulates in Africa. Consequently, little is left over for those below ambassadorial rank.

In India, sixty-four United States Information officers have to share $4,700. In Holland at a seminar held some time ago for leading Dutch newspaper editors, the United States embassy organizers had to tell their guests during the luncheon break that they could have either two glasses of beer or two glasses of gin; and to add to their embarrassment, the waiters had to be instructed to serve not more than one slice of meat per person because the available hospitality allocation did not run to more. As one old "State" hand put it, "The United States gives away billions of dollars worth of tractors, shipyards and steel plants, but it won't pay for a square meal. People quickly forget the former but not the latter."

Many Congressmen are blissfully unaware of the situation and gaily expect to be lavishly entertained on their foreign forays out of their diplomatic representatives' "booze allowance."

On the whole, Foreign Service officers take these visitations philosophically, although they do find it difficult sometimes to stifle doubts about the usefulness and high cost of the more flamboyant Congressional junkets. They were somewhat taken aback, for example, to learn in the summer of 1962 that one Congressman was heading for Europe to study equality of opportunity for Continental women. He began his researches at the elegant Crillon Hotel in Paris, later moved to a fashionable seaside resort in Greece and when criticism of his trip mounted in the United States, eventually announced in Madrid that the real purpose of his tour was to study the Common Market. Spain, of course, happens to be outside the Common Market.

Doubts where Congress is concerned, however, are never expressed except in the strictest privacy. Foreign

Service officers know that visiting legislators come in all shapes, sizes and temperaments and that a quiet chat over a glass of Scotch or Bourbon after an official reception can do more for a policy on Capitol Hill than a closely reasoned situation report running into thousands of words. They also realize that a quiet chat is sometimes not enough to generate good will and a bipartisan approach to foreign affairs. Legislators, after all, are like other men. They want to be out and about when the day's investigating is done, to shop and to visit theaters, art galleries and night clubs. Moreover, many of them are human enough to be celebrity hunters.

This presents no special problems to Foreign Service officers in places like Bonn. Dr. Adenauer always finds time to receive visiting Senators. Indeed, he is deeply hurt if a member of the Senate passes through town without looking him up.

In other capitals, it is not so easy. American diplomats at the embassy in Rome, for example, know that one of the first things practically every visitor from Capitol Hill requests on arrival is a private audience with the Pope. They could reply that they are technically accredited to the Italian Republic and not to the Holy See, an independent state in international law, with which by the sovereign will of her people the United States has no direct diplomatic relations, but since they have no wish to appear difficult, they spare their legislators a lecture on the niceties of the law of nations and try to meet the request by all sorts of devious and obscure means.

The London embassy, too, has its special problems. There they usually arise from requests to see the Queen.

Fortunately, as one American diplomat put it, the Queen is "very understanding."

Equally understanding, so it appears, was Sir Winston Churchill before he retired from active politics. For many years following the Second World War few members of the Senate or the House were content to pass through London without meeting him and, if possible, having their photograph taken shaking his hand. Among the more irreverent American diplomats at the embassy in Grosvenor Square these requests came to be dubbed Operation "Seeking Statesmanship by Association." Certainly it gave the more obscure members of Congress the chance to insert into their speeches now and then phrases like, "As I said to Churchill when we discussed this question. . ."

In short, United States Foreign Service officers have a very clear picture of their place in the scheme of things. Above all, they know that their effectiveness depends, in the final analysis, on the relationship between the Secretary of State and the President. The Constitution may make him the President's Grand Vizier in foreign policy, but the President does not live in the State Department, and in the White House Presidents are apt to surround themselves with special assistants, advisors extraordinary and policy planners plenipotentiary of their own. The men at "State" wish sometimes that the Secretary of State could spend more time in Washington, nearer the President—a target which both Christian Herter and Dean Rusk set themselves on first taking office and which has eluded both of them. The inflationary spiral of crises has piled on the miles. In his first year of office, Herter flew

77

more miles than Dulles in his first twelve months, and Rusk's total caps Herter's. The average annual flying mileage of a Secretary of State at the present time stands in the region of 100,000 miles.

Still the State Department lives in hopes. One day it feels sure, the ingenuity and resourcefulness of the American aircraft industry will be equal to inventing the miracle plane that would be the answer to many prayers: an aircraft capable of taking off from Washington without the Secretary of State.

6:

Diplomacy
and the
Press: I

THE UNITED STATES INFORMATION SERVICE AT AMERICAN
embassies and legations throughout the world goes to
great lengths to ensure that the press gets the facts right,
and rarely misses a chance of issuing a handout.

When Mrs. Luce arrived in Italy in 1953 to take up her
post as U. S. ambassador there, the Information Office
in Rome circulated the following statement to the Italian
press:

*Will you kindly note for your files or morgue the correct
spelling of her name:*

MRS.	CLARE	BOOTHE	LUCE
(not *Miss*)	(no *i*)	(ends in *e*)	

When Mrs. Luce's name is incorrectly spelled, she is sometimes wrongly identified as Miss Claire Luce, the professional stage and television actress.

Despite all this, one Italian picture magazine adorned its cover with a photograph of Miss Claire Luce, in the role of Cleopatra, being passionately embraced by Antony, and the caption underneath proclaimed unequivocally, "The New American ambassador."

The magazine was soon sold out.

7:

British
Diplomacy's
Headquarters

THE BUILDING THAT HOUSES THE FOREIGN OFFICE IN Downing street opposite "No. 10," is not one of London's landmarks. Its solid, Mid-Victorian façade has little architectural merit and looks disappointingly unpretentious. A more imposing design submitted by that great church architect Sir George Gilbert Scott did not find favor with Lord Palmerston, who felt that it would make the Foreign Office look like "a flamboyant Gothic wedding cake." Sir George's labors, however, were not entirely wasted. His plans for the Foreign Office were eventually accepted for St. Pancras railway station.

The interior of the Foreign Office, too, is apt to produce

a feeling of anticlimax. The corridors look somewhat drab, especially on a rainy day; most of the offices seem overcrowded; and only a broad, sweeping staircase leading to the first floor adds a touch of grandeur. Instead of the heavy perfume of intrigue which most visitors half expect, there is a musty smell of records and files; and instead of hatching devilishly cunning Machiavellian plots, everyone seems to be fighting desperately against being swamped by the flood of dispatches, memoranda and telegrams ceaselessly pouring in from all over the world. The nerve center of British diplomacy, in fact, appears to be singularly devoid of glamour and drama.

Yet "being something in the Foreign Office" has its compensations. Whether your father is a dustman or your mother a charwoman, you are, by virtue of your job, a gentleman. Every hostess in town will welcome you. You will be dined and wined in all the best houses. And overworked though you may be, you have the satisfaction of knowing that you belong to one of the world's most exclusive corps d'elite.

For the number of those privileged to look after Britain's relations with the rest of the world is surprisingly small, considering the complexities of the job. Of the total Foreign Service strength of about 3,800, which includes messengers, lift men and clerks, only the seven hundred members of the senior, administrative branch are in effect concerned with molding British policy. It is almost entirely from their ranks that consuls, ambassadors, departmental heads and Assistant Under Secretaries are chosen, and since home and foreign appointments are mutually interchangeable—no appointment is usually held for longer than three years—there are seldom more than two hundred members of the senior branch available at any given moment, to hold the fort in Downing Street.

The head of this select band of brothers is the Permanent Under Secretary of State, Britain's top professional diplomat, in whose office all the many strands of foreign policy come together. He treats his colleagues as he would members of his club, discouraging even the junior Secretaries on the threshold of their careers from calling him "Sir"; yet there is very little he cannot do when it comes to promotions, transfers, appointments and and decisions on policy.

Of course, like any civil servant, he is subject to the political head of his department, in his case Her Majesty's Principal Secretary of State for Foreign Affairs, or Foreign Secretary for short. And there are also four other political appointees in the Foreign Office, two Ministers of State and two Parliamentary Under Secretaries, whose duties consist in relieving the Foreign Secretary of much of his parliamentary work, of representing him at the lengthier kind of international conference like the United Nations' General Assembly, and of saving his digestion by taking his place at innumerable diplomatic cocktail parties and dinners.

But Foreign Secretaries, Ministers of State and Parliamentary Under Secretaries come and go. Their hold on office depends on such ephemeral things as votes of confidence in the House of Commons and election results, while the Permanent Under Secretary of State goes on forever—or at least until he reaches retiring age. He takes the long view, and it is sometimes his painful duty to point out to his political masters that plans for curing the world's ills, devised in the heat of an election battle, do not necessarily accord with the facts of international life.

His views are of course always presented in the constitutionally correct form of "advice." But Foreign Secretaries are not supposed to disagree too frequently with the advice they are offered. On the whole, they are expected to content themselves with "stimulating" the work of the "Office," a less positive form of activity which Permanent Under Secretaries, past and present, never fail to praise in their political superiors.

Below the Permanent Under Secretary, the Foreign Office is organized into just over three dozen departments —Northern, American, Far Eastern, Western Organizations, Cultural Relations, Finance, Security, and so on. There is, however, no central policy planning department, and if the visitor inquires how the Foreign Office manages to get along without a department which plays so prominent a role in the organization of most other foreign ministries, he is likely to receive the astonishing reply, "Because there is no such thing as a British foreign policy."

The Foreign Office professional distrusts generalizations and all the fashionable talk about the global approach. The Americans, he realizes, cannot help that kind of thing, and he has learned to listen patiently to blueprints for such colossal, world-wide policy projects as "peripheral defence," "containment of world communism" and "massive retaliation," hoping that he will in due course be able to get down to business. As for the rest, he leaves cosmic diplomacy to editors and political columnists, shrugs indulgently when weekly periodicals like *The Economist, The Spectator* or *The New Statesman and Nation* accuse the Foreign Office of drift and living from hand to mouth, and points with just the smallest suspicious of malice to the unfortunate case of Mr. Shepilov who, after many happy years of carefree political punditry in the columns of Pravda, was at last allowed to have a go at the real thing and then made such a mess of running the Soviet Foreign Ministry that he had to be unceremoniously dismissed after only a few brief months in office.

The men viewing the world from the fastnesses of the Foreign Office prefer to cope with each situation as it crops up. Trying to do business with nearly one hundred sovereign nations in five different continents according to a preordained pattern of universal application seems to them, as Theodore Roosevelt said about dealing with Colombians, "like nailing currant jelly to the wall." That way there is bound to be a muddle sooner or later. And the best method they know of avoiding a muddle is to muddle through.

The truth of the matter is, of course, that Britain had the broad pattern of her policy dictated to her by geography and history centuries ago. Basic alternative policies like neutrality or a system of alliances may at times be an issue in other countries; in Britain there is no such choice. As a tiny island a few miles off the coast of a turbulent continent, she cannot allow any power hostile to her to dominate Europe, and as a nation with world-wide interests, dependent on trade and commerce for her survival, she must see to it that the seven seas remain open.

Everyone who belongs to the Foreign Service is supposed to have absorbed this lesson into his bloodstream and not to need a central planning department to spell it out for him. Otherwise, he is likely to be of little use in any of the departments of the Foreign Office.

The typical head of a department is in his late thirties or early forties, usually a Counselor in rank. Behind him lie periods of service as Third, Second and First Secretary, and before him stretches the prospect of advancement to Minister, or Assistant Under Secretary, and possibly, if he is lucky, to the Permanent Under Secretaryship of State.

His main private worry, however, is likely to be how soon he can hope to get another appointment abroad—especially if he has recently returned from foreign parts. For, after leading a tax free existence, sustained by rent, cost of living and entertainment allowance, it is no joke to find oneself stripped of all diplomatic emoluments right down to a counselor's basic pay (£2,000-£2,600) and at the same time exposed to the icy blast of British rates of income tax.

His twenty-odd years in the Foreign Service will have included at least three or four two- to three-year stints at posts abroad, and he will have seen enough of the world to have learned, not only that all foreigners are not rascals, but also that—contrary to what many do-gooders are fond of preaching—all people, when it comes down to it, are not basically alike. He looks, in fact, what he is—a man of the world who has smelt the smells and seen the sights. And as he muses over the financial sacrifices that service in the Foreign Office seems to entail, he will draw what consolation he can from the fact that as head of a department he enjoys at least one privilege denied to his inferiors, an office of his own. His two assistants, usually First Secretaries in rank, share an adjoining room, and the handful of junior secretaries who form the bulk of his department have to make do as best they can in the cramped and often chaotic quarters of the "Third Room."

Yet there—as is the way of the world—most of the hard work is done. The "Third Room" or rather "Third Rooms," Counselors and upwards explain complacently, are "the backbone of the Foreign Office."

Let us suppose then that among the more than ten thousand telegrams that pass through the Foreign Office every month—many of them running to hundreds of words—there is one from Her Britannic Majesty's ambassador in Bangkok. It is "unbuttoned" in the Code Room— very few telegram these days are sent "en clair" and not in cipher—carefully locked away in a red leather dispatch box and taken by messenger to the "Third Room" of the appropriate department, in this case the South-East Asia Department, where it is handed to the Junior Secretary who usually deals with Thailand.

Everything, you note, begins at the bottom, and it can end there, too. For it is entirely within the discretion of the Junior Secretary whether he consults his seniors or drafts and dispatches an "instruction" on his own. He is supposed to know enough about the "office" to be capable of judging how much he can take on himself. And if he chances his arm, his "instruction" has the full weight of the Foreign Office behind it, just as much as an instruction sent by the Permanent Under Secretary of State—no matter to whom it is addressed. "The Foreign Office," the visitor is told proudly," is not bound by rigid rules of hierarchical procedure, like most other foreign ministries. Why, if he felt it to be appropriate, a junior secretary could even dispatch instructions for war to be declared." To which, if the visitor should show symptoms of panic on discovering that the question of war and peace might be left in the hands of a cheerful pink-faced Third Secretary in his rising twenties, the soothing comment is immediately added, "Of course, should a declaration of war appear somewhat abrupt and unreasonable to the ambassador at the other end, he for his part is entitled to delay delivering it and in the meantime to ask for "clarification" and "further instructions."

Certainly a Junior Secretary is expected not to waste his superiors' time by trying to "cover" himself, and "passing the buck" is severely frowned upon. But heaven help him if his judgment is faulty. He can abandon all hope of ever being posted to Paris, Rome, Washington or any of the more glamorous and important of the world's capitals. The best he can look forward to in his future career is a long succession of consular posts in obscure, isolated and uncomfortable corners of Africa and Asia.

After a quick glance at the Bangkok telegram, our Junior Secretary decides that the point it raises is one on which his seniors might like to be consulted. What the ambassador wants to know is whether, the next time he sees the Thai Foreign Minister, he should protest against the increasingly anti-Western and pro-Chinese Communist attitude of one or two leading members of the Thai government, or whether he should continue to hold his fire.

There are, the man in the "Third Room" realizes, arguments on both sides. On the one hand, Thailand as a member of the South-East Asia Pact is Britain's ally and may resent a vigorous protest. On the other hand, a country where the same set of politicians collaborated with the Japanese during the war and with the Western Powers afterwards, equally happily, obviously does not take the same jaundiced view of changes in allegiance that may be held elsewhere; and since it is an accepted tradition in Thai politics for cabinet members to intrigue against one another and pursue conflicting policies, the Foreign Minister may even welcome a protest as a means of scoring off his colleagues. Moreover, there are the interests of the United States and the attitudes of the Asian and Pacific Commonwealth countries to be taken into account.

Still, delicate though the problem is, it is up to the Junior Secretary to start the ball rolling. After a word with a colleague in the American Department and a lengthy telephone conversation with the Commonwealth Relations Office, he drafts a "minute" on a "foolscap jacket," suggesting an appropriate reply to the ambassador, and sends it in to one of the assistant heads of his department. He, in his turn, may add a sheet or two of comments of his own before passing it on the head of the department. From there, the "jacket" wanders up to one of the Assistant Under Secretaries—each Assistant Under Secretary supervises the work of a number of departments—and eventually finds its way on to the desk of the Permanent Under Secretary of State.

That high official can either give the go-ahead, or send the "minute" with all the additions and observations it has gathered on its way up, right down the line again for "elaboration," "condensation" or "clarification." Or he can send it up one stage higher still to his political chief, the Foreign Secretary—which he invariably does if he has reason to believe that the Foreign Secretary might otherwise lose touch with the work of the "office."

In this instance, there are two good reasons. In the first place, the Foreign Secretary and the American Secretary of State are about to meet to thrash out the problem of Anglo-American differences in Asia, and any action by Britain in that part of the world, taken without the knowledge and express consent of the Foreign Secretary, might obviously embarrass him in his coming talks with his American colleague. Secondly, the Parliamentary Under Secretary in the House of Commons has warned of possible trouble from one of the more querulous Opposition M.P.'s, who has recently returned from an extensive Asian tour. Apparently the M.P. was deeply shocked to discover that some high Thai officials derive a comfortable income from brothels and the opium trade and is now thinking of raising the question of how the Foreign Office selects its allies.

As a professional diplomat, the Permanent Under-Secretary of course deplores the tendency, prevalent among some M.P.s, of wanting to organize the concert of nations as though it were a meeting of parochial churchwardens; but these emotional, irrational parliamentary squalls can, he knows, be tricky, and he is out to protect his political chief. After all, the Foreign Office, like every Department of State, is in the last resort dependent on Parliament, and if the Foreign Secretary gets into trouble there, which is all too easy if he is not properly briefed, and the House of Commons senses that he is not on top of his job, the Foreign Office as a whole is bound to suffer.

The Foreign Secretary, whose engagement book between now and next Christmas looks like a subway timetable for the rush hour, casts a cursory glance over the "foolscap jacket" and its contents. There is no point in his doing any more. For even if he had time to read it carefully, where would he find the time to think about it? And so he calls a meeting of all concerned in his office, an enormous corner room on the first floor with five French windows facing out on St. James's Park and Horse Guard's Parade. "Best office in London," one of the Foreign Secretary's personal staff whispers. "Not that anybody notices it, except on the day when there's the Trooping of the Color ceremony. And then we have a big buffet here for our guests." The Foreign Secretary's broad, red-topped desk sits massively opposite a marble fireplace above which an indifferent portrait of a scrupulously vacant-looking George III surveys the scene.

There are plenty of easy chairs, all covered in red leather, dotted around the room, and the atmosphere at these brief policy meetings almost suggests the smoking room of one of the better London clubs. Admittedly the professionals will call their political head "sir," but everyone sits or stands about as it suits him. The arguments for and against lodging a protest in Bangkok are neatly brought out. After the deliberation, noting the wide measure of agreement among his professional advisors, the Foreign Secretary reaches the decision that the ambassador should hold his fire and let matters ride for the time being.

Which in all probability was exactly what the Junior Secretary in his "Third Room" had proposed to begin with.

Even at night and over the weekend the Foreign Office must be geared for action, for weekends have long since ceased to be sacred, and world events no longer march in step with London office hours.

From New York the Head of the British Delegation to the United Nations may require "urgent guidance" on what line he should take in an emergency session of the Security Council. It may be only nine o'clock in the evening there, but in London it will be 2 A.M.

From the Far East one of Her Majesty's representatives may report "a serious incident" that has taken place at noon local time, but in London it will still be an hour before dawn.

The man who copes with these nocturnal crises is one of the team of four Resident Clerks, usually a Second Secretary in rank, who has reached the ripe age of thirty or thereabouts. In the daytime he is just one of threescore assistant heads of departments, but between dusk and dawn he is all the departments of the Foreign Office rolled into one, the pivot of Britain's world-wide diplomatic network.

Talking to him in his set of rooms on top of the Foreign Office is rather like trying to sustain a coherent conversation with a policeman on traffic duty. No sooner have you begun to congratulate him on the magnificent view of the Mall from his window than his attention is likely to be claimed by the latest dispatch from Washington, an angry Soviet protest about something or other— as a rule these can safely be left over until next morning— or a telegram from the British Minister in a riot-torn Eastern principality asking for arrangements to be made for the evacuation of British civilians.

The telephone, a green instrument fitted with a scrambling device to prevent eavesdropping, is never silent for very long. It may be a British consul in Italy asking him to contact the relatives of a British tourist injured in a car accident. It may be the War Office wanting him to issue an emergency passport to a woman about to be flown out to her sick soldier son serving in the Far East. Or it may be "No. 10," where the P.M. is about to receive the president of one of the smaller Latin American republics. Apparently the P.M. remembers seeing a photograph of the president surrounded by a bevy of beautiful young ladies in some American magazine a long time ago. As far as he recalls, the caption underneath it read, "The President as a family man," and he is wondering whether a reference to the joys of family life would make an appropriate opening gambit to put his guest at ease.

The Resident Clerk contacts one of the First Secretaries in the American Department at his home, and after a lengthy consultation rings back "No. 10." The magazine in which the article appeared was—so it seems—being highly critical of the president, and "family man" was pointedly put in quotation marks because the president, a confirmed bachelor, is well known in his own country as a ladies' man who likes to surround himself with glamorous members of the opposite sex. Any reference by the P.M. to the joys of family life might therefore easily lead to misunderstanding.

In return for having his nights disturbed, a Resident Clerk receives a "clerking" allowance of £75 a year— subject to income tax—and the privilege of snatching what sleep he can in a large mahogany bed which once belonged to one of Queen Victoria's Prime Ministers, the third Marquess of Salisbury. In that bed was first read Marshal Bulganin's note informing Britain, at the height of the Suez crisis, that London and Paris were within atomic missile range.

But Resident Clerks are not given to panicking, even in the small, gray hours of the morning, and they soon learn to take the inconveniences of their job in their stride.

When on duty, a Resident Clerk is not allowed to leave the Foreign Office building for one second, and even moving about within the building, from one room to another, entails as much preparation as going abroad does for an ordinary mortal.

First, he picks up the bulky bunch of keys which open and lock the various Foreign Office despatch boxes and many of its safes. Secondly, he makes sure he has with him the bulky file which gives the movements of all Cabinet Ministers and senior Foreign Office officials. It tells him that one of the Ministers of State is attending a musical soiree at the Austrian embassy, that the Foreign Secretary is traveling north to address a political meeting in his constituency, and that the Permanent Under Secretary is spending the night with his brother in the country.

And finally, before he goes anywhere, the Resident Clerk always rings up the central switchboard to tell them where he can be found. A thoughtful government has installed telephones in all the places that he is likely to visit, the dining room, the sitting room and the kitchen.

There is even a telephone right outside the bathroom. The poor man in fact, never seems to get a moment's peace. But, as one experienced Resident Clerk once pointed out to a visitor, "there is no crisis that can't wait for a minute or two while I finish brushing my teeth."

Quite a few foreign governments, one feels, would give up sending Britain rude notes if they had any inkling of the circumstances in which some of their carefully drafted, pompously worded missives were received.

8:

Diplomacy and the Press: II

WHEN GENERAL EISENHOWER BECAME NATO'S FIRST supreme Commander in Europe in 1950, he worked hard to enlist the support of the press in his efforts to promote good will and understanding among the Western allies. On his initiative, groups of journalists from the various NATO countries were regularly invited to visit his headquarters at Marly near Paris, where he and the senior officers of his staff were always ready to receive them.

Needless to say, these tours were very popular with the press—for what could be pleasanter than to combine a serious study of the international situation with a visit to Paris?

But of course the situation had its drawbacks. Early in 1952, for example, a group of American editors flew into Paris late one afternoon, discovered that NATO had laid on no appointments for them until the following day, and promptly decided to investigate the Place Pigalle.

Naturally, some of the members of the party did not feel their best next morning when they were entertained by General Eisenhower and his staff. There was one editor, in particular, who, though perfectly amiable, just could not stop talking.

All went well, however, until he suddenly found himself standing next to the French Admiral Lemonnier, who was then Deputy Supreme Commander on the naval side. He glanced at Lemonnier's uniform and was obviously wondering to what nationality and service its wearer belonged. But his compelling urge to talk would not let him remain silent for very long.

"General," he announced at the first opportunity, "you Italians have done a splendid job of recovery."

One of Admiral Lemonnier's aides tried to interrupt, but the editor was beyond anyone's reach, in a blissful cotton wool world of his own where social faux-pas were unknown. Nothing could stem the flow of his words.

"Why, take the Fiat works, for instance. At the end of the war they were a dreadful shambles. But look at the fine little cars they turn out now. A splendid job of recovery, General."

When he stopped at last, the silence that followed seemed long and oppressive. It was obviously too late to intervene and politely attempt to change the conversation.

"Your discourse has been most interesting," Admiral

Lemonnier said eventually, choosing his words with great care. "I have only two comments to make! One: I am French, not Italian, and two"—here his voice exploded—"I am not a general; I'm an admiral!"

The editor was the only person in the room who was not startled by this outburst. "Admiral," he said genially, "you French have done a splendid job of recovery. Why, take the Renault works, for instance. . ."

9:

Moscow's
Militant
Diplomats

THE FIRST PEOPLE'S COMMISSAR FOR FOREIGN AFFAIRS
after the Bolshevik Revolution was Trotsky, and his
first official act was to stroll into what had until recently
been the Czarist Foreign Ministry, take a look around
and announce casually, "I will issue some revolutionary
proclamations to the peoples of the world and then close
up the joint."

Like many official Soviet statements made subsequently,
it turned out to be incorrect. The Soviet Foreign Ministry
today is one of the largest, if not the largest, in the
world.

But that is perhaps the least important aspect of

Trotsky's rash pronouncement. Far more significant is the disdain, the contempt, that it shows for diplomacy, for in this he reflects an attitude which to a greater or lesser extent has been shared by the leaders of Soviet Russia from the earliest revolutionary days down to the present. In their view, the traditional ways of doing business between sovereign states contradicts the essential spirit of their creed. Marxism teaches them that capitalist society will collapse and bourgeois forms crumble. Why, then, use outdated capitalist methods like diplomacy? Why bother to have dealings with other governments at all? Why not go over their heads and deal directly with ordinary men and women in other lands to aid and stimulate the world revolution that is bound to come sooner or later?

To Trotsky, the victory of revolutionary socialism seemed just around the corner, and he therefore regarded the ministry under his charge not only as wicked but also as useless and unnecessary.

On his first morning he assembled the complete staff he had inherited from the previous regime and told "those who are for us" to go to the left and "those who are against us" to go to the right. The professional diplomats, the clerks, secretaries and archivists stepped to the right in a body, and Trotsky found himself left with a handful of cleaners, porters and guards. He was delighted. His plans for dismantling Russias's Foreign Service were proceeding at a more cracking pace than he had hoped for, and to complete his first day's work he sacked most of Russia's ambassadors and ministers abroad.

Unfortunately for him, the world revolution he anticipated failed to materialize; governments and regimes which he confidently expected to topple remained firmly in the saddle; and, what was worse, the Soviet Union was compelled to seek ways and means of establishing diplomatic relations with them, unless it wanted to go into voluntary purdah.

It was a bitter disappointment, but there was no choice. The Foreign Service had to be rebuilt. The Soviet leaders, however, had no intention of creating a diplomatic service along traditional lines. Their retreat was tactical. Their basic attitude toward diplomacy had not changed, and they used their new service accordingly.

Soviet embassies abroad became primarily centers of propaganda. Their main function, particularly in the nineteen-twenties, was to foment trouble and spread the gospel of world revolution. One Soviet representative traveled with suitcases stuffed full of communist propaganda tracts to be distributed around the country where he was accredited. Another delivered inflammatory speeches. And a third started directing the operations of the local revolutionary movement before he had even presented his credentials to his host government. All three were expelled and sent back to Russia with the minimum of ceremony, and it gradually dawned on the Soviet leaders that diplomacy and underground political activity were incompatible, at least when the link was discovered.

It was a point the People's Commissariat for Foreign Affairs had tried to impress on its masters from the very beginning, but then it counted for little in the Soviet scheme of things. It had no say in the formulation of foreign policy, which was decided by the Party's Politburo.

It was rarely consulted, and at times not even informed of policy decisions. It was no more than a tool to be used or ignored as convenience demanded. Its chief, the People's Commissar for Foreign Affairs, may have been addressed by foreign ambassadors as "His Excellency" in accordance with diplomatic protocol, but in the Party hierarchy where the power lay, he was a man of little account. In fact, with the exception of Molotov, none of the People's Commissars, or Ministers as they were later called, has ever belonged to inner councils of the all-powerful Party. They have all been, to quote the description which Mr. Kruschev gave in public of his Foreign Minister Gromyko, "mere bureaucrats."

The man charged with rebuilding Russia's Foreign Service—Trotsky had become Commissar for War after his drastic pruning of the diplomatic establishment—was Georgii Chicherin, a shy, timid man who did not care how he dressed, a scholar of considerable merit, a hypochrondriac and an aristocrat. He had broken with his family and joined the Bolsheviks long before the Revolution, but according to his writings, the decision had not been easy for him. He had reached it only after long and intensive study and thought, and his health had been undermined. Although Lenin picked him as Commissar because he had once been an archivist in the Czar's Foreign Ministry, he never thought he was tough enough for the job. Indeed, on one occasion after the Politburo had decided on a particularly ruthless course of action, Lenin remarked casually that it would send Chicherin to bed for a few months as soon as he heard of it, and he soon put Litvinov into the Commissariat as No. 2, to give the department more backbone.

Under such circumstances even a tougher character than Chicherin would have had a difficult time making the country's creaking diplomatic machine work, and it is not surprising that the Commissariat in the nineteen-twenties enjoyed a reputation among foreign diplomats for unparalleled inefficiency.

The department was run by a four-man collegium, over which Chicherin presided, which was served by a secretariat divided into functional sections—administration, personnel, press, economics and law—and two geographical sections, simply called East and West. The East covered the Near East, Africa, the Middle East and Far East; and the Western section dealt with Central Europe, the Balkans, Scandinavia and a subsection known as Anglo-Roman in which in a lordly fashion Britain, the United States, France, Italy, Spain and all of Latin America had been lumped together.

Pay was low—lower than in other government departments—and the five hundred to six hundred men and women who were eventually recruited could hardly be called a happy team. Chicherin and Litvinov did not get on well together, and Chicherin made no secret of the poor opinion he had of his staff. He insisted on tackling most jobs himself, not only drafting and typing diplomatic notes but sealing and posting them personally. As a result, it often took months to get an answer even to a routine inquiry out of the Commissariat. Moreover, Chicherin had the habit of mislaying important documents, and since he disliked modern office equipment and distrusted filing, days were often wasted in searching for them. His hours became more and more erratic. Foreign diplomats would be asked to call on him for an interview in the middle of the night, and if they were unlucky, they would find upon arrival that he had locked himself away for a few hours to play Mozart on his piano. Yet few foreign diplomats denied his skill, given the conditions under which he had to work. A brilliant linguist, he had a sharp mind, a quick wit and a formidable knowledge of history. Anyone crossing swords with him had to be well briefed. In fact, all he lacked was power.

If conditions at head office were chaotic, they were even worse at the embassies and legations abroad. Admittedly, Soviet diplomats were no longer supposed to act officially as standard bearers of the Revolution, but the Politburo, the Secret Police and other organs of the Party and state had their own people in each mission abroad who were a law unto themselves. They received their instructions without reference to the Foreign Commissariat and ignored Chicherin's orders. When he protested to the Politburo he was usually told to mind his own business. Moreover, many Soviet ambassadors were senior to Chicherin in the Party hierarchy and took no notice of their nominal chief.

Not that this can have sweetened their lives for long. Sooner or later all of them discovered that diplomacy and Communism are like water and oil; they do not mix. If a Soviet diplomat reported back on events and people as they were, and not as they ought to be according to Marxist doctrine, he ran the risk of being accused of "reactionary deviationism." If he reported as the Party doctrinaires expected him to he cannot have failed to realize that he was denying his country information vital to intelligent and effective policy formulation. As a Communist, he knew that the end justified lying, cheating and double-dealing; as

106

a diplomat, he knew that the tactics he was from time to time ordered to employ created nothing but suspicion and distrust and destroyed all hope of building good relations between the Soviet Union and the outside world.

The dilemma was constantly with him, and the strain was often immense. For many years the only way out, especially in the late nineteen-twenties and early nineteen-thirties, was to defect, but this only made matters worse for those who remained behind. For Stalin, who had by then become the master of the Kremlin, had a simple remedy: more supervision, more Secret Policemen in every embassy and legation. In some missions there were more OGPU men than diplomats. Members of the diplomatic staff were made to live in apartments and houses where the security people could keep an eye on them and their families. They were discouraged from mixing with the natives. In fact, by the middle nineteen-thirties, when Litvinov, who had succeeded Chicherin, was talking of little else but the delights of international cooperation and collective security and was asking the world to recognize that peace was indivisible, many Soviet missions had virtually become diplomatic ghettoes. Cooped up and deprived of ordinary social contacts, their inmates not infrequently took to quarreling among themselves, and there was a succession of sordid scandals. Morale in the Soviet Foreign Service had never been so low.

At the beginning of 1939, when Molotov took over from Litvinov, to perform the most amazing volte-face in Soviet diplomacy by his signing of a pact with Hitler, he set out to remedy the sorry situation not by resolving his diplomatic brethren's dilemma—for him there was none—

but by recruiting a new breed of diplomats—efficient, capable, ruthless, tough, and unquestioningly loyal to all and any orders from the Kremlin.

He was admirably suited for the task. Lenin may once have dismissed him as "the best filing clerk in Russia," and Karl Radek, who was executed in one of Stalin's purges, may have nicknamed him "Stone Bottom," but Churchill, who had many an encounter with him during the war, saw him as "a man of outstanding ability and cold-blooded ruthlessness." In his view, "he was, above all men, fitted to be the agent of the policy of an incalculable machine."

Molotov wanted the Soviet Foreign Service to be staffed by others like himself. The happy-go-lucky inefficiency, the waywardness, the downright chaos, which had always been a feature of Russian administration under both Czarism and Communism, had to be eradicated. Everything had to be just so. With his pince-nez and pedantic fussiness which caused Western diplomats to refer to him as "Auntie Moll," he pursued his goal with the determined air of a maiden aunt who could not stand untidiness, and he succeeded.

Of course, he was lucky. At the time he took over the Foreign Ministry, the first crop of young men who had been educated entirely under the Soviet regime were leaving the universities and academies to begin their careers. They had been too young to play an active part in the Revolution. For them the bitter ideological battles and arguments of that period were subjects that had to be studied in order to pass examinations. Their passions and emotions were not involved. Their main concern, like

Molotov's, was to make things work. They were ideal material for the kind of Foreign Service he wanted.

The right type, once he had caught Molotov's eye, could expect meteoric promotion. After graduating from the Institute of Economics, Andrei Gromyko had for a while lectured at one of the academies that were mass-producing administrators and technicians. He had been in the Foreign Ministry for only a year when Molotov sent him to the Soviet embassy in Washington in no less a position than that of Counselor. He did not know a word of English, but that was no serious obstacle for one of the new Molotov breed. Gromyko set to work with the embassy interpreter and a battery of books. In due course, he mastered the language so well that when later on, at the United Nations and at disarmament conferences, he queried points of detail in the official translation, he was usually found to be right.

He had also never been abroad before he was sent to Washington, but that did not worry the new Soviet diplomat, for in a sense he never left the Soviet Union even when stationed outside it. He worked away at his desk absorbing massive briefs and writing voluminous reports and at the end of the day rarely went anywhere but his home. Certainly Gromyko at that time hardly mixed with Americans, except on his regular Saturday afternoon trip to one of Washington's picture houses. Yet four years later he was promoted to Chargé d'Affaires, and a few months afterward he became Soviet ambassador to the United States. At the time he was only thirty-five.

After the war, the world saw more products of Molotov's recruiting policy. They all seemed to be cast in the same mold. They functioned with extreme skill and precision in exact accordance with their instructions from Moscow. They hurled passionate insults one moment and exuded charm the next. They stomped out of conferences in a towering rage one day and returned a day later as if nothing had happened. Their speeches were sweetly reasonable and rudely obstructionist in turn. Their own feelings throughout these remarkable performances never showed through. They remained remote and had few social contacts. They were the utterly dedicated instruments of "an incalculable machine."

At the head office in Moscow, Molotov's reorganizing zeal was hard at work. The Foreign Ministry was streamlined, chains of command were redefined, and eventually everyone was moved into a brand-new headquarters, a vast skyscraper that looks rather like an overornate wedding cake.

No doubt the idea was to provide the Foreign Minister and his staff with a setting that was thought to be in keeping with the Soviet Union's increased importance in the world, but foreign diplomats sent to Moscow soon discover that there is no point in going there if they want the answers to really weighty questions. The Foreign Ministry's corridors are brightly lighted but lifeless, and its senior officials, though always courteous and pleasant, are past masters in the art of side-stepping direct questions.

Real power, indeed, still lies where it always has—in the inner councils of the Party. All the reforms and reorganizations effected by Molotov before his enforced retirement from active politics cannot hide that fact; and as if to underline it, the new Foreign Ministry is well away from the center of Moscow and the Kremlin.

Moreover, Krushchev's contempt for his professional diplomats appears to be hardly less than that of the early revolutionary leaders. Admittedly, he has ordered them to get out and about and not to stay closeted in their embassies. Their pay and allowances are good, in marked contrast with prewar days, and no expense is spared for entertainments. Ambassadors, he realizes, can do a good job of public relations if their special qualities suit the conditions and atmosphere of the country to which they are sent. In the United States, public figures plainly must have the gift of the bright smile and the ready handshake; and so as one of his recent ambassadors to Washington he chose Michael Menshikov, whose untiring efforts at cheerfulness quickly won him the title "Smiling Mike." In France, the great thing obviously is culture, so some of the Soviet ambassadors in Paris have been men whose profound knowledge of French literature even the most learned French Academician is bound to treat as a subtle compliment to his country.

When it comes to policy making, however, Krushchev wants no interference from his diplomats. They are there to do as they are told, and although he expects them to don dinner jackets and all the other trappings of the capitalist social round when occasion demands, he himself refuses to conform and does not take kindly to criticism of his earthy brand of behavior. When Shepilov, the former Pravda editor turned Foreign Minister, voiced the thought that he occasionally felt embarrassed by Krushchev's rather uncouth manners on foreign trips, he found his brief period of ministerial glory abruptly terminated.

At the same time, the realities of the nuclear age make Krushchev more dependent on his diplomats than any previous Soviet leader. Stalin in the nineteen-thirties may have thought he could afford the luxury of having his diplomats virtually locked up in their embassies and so incapable of sending him a scrap of accurate information on what was going on around them; Krushchev must know what is happening. An accurate picture of other people's strength, mood and morale is essential to his policy making. Misinformation can lead to miscalculation; miscalculation, to a nuclear holocaust.

His problem is this: Can he find men who can correctly gauge the impulses and motives of societies which Marxism has taught them to regard as corrupt and decaying? In recent years the Soviet Foreign Ministry has taken on droves of young men who have done well in the universities or academies and sent them out to the embassies as attachés. Once abroad, they spend most of their time simply absorbing the atmosphere—going to party conventions, attending Congress or Parliament, visiting universities, listening to lectures and debates, and saying very little themselves.

It is a first tentative move to grapple with the problem, and those in charge of recruitment obviously hope to solve it by the old, traditional Russian steam-roller methods. The numbers taken on seem far in excess of any possible future staff requirements, but since they are all on probation, those who fail to make the grade can be easily weeded out. Even so, there remains the question, Will they find enough?

10:

The Gentle Art
of Negotiation

"THE SECRET OF NEGOTIATION," FRANCOIS DE CALLIERES,
one of the most distinguished diplomats in Louis XIV's
service, wrote more than two and a half centuries ago, "is
to harmonize the real interests of the parties concerned."
He also wrote, "Menaces always do harm to negotiation."

His great work, *De la Manière de Négocier Avec les
Souverains*, is still regarded as a classic among diplomats,
but many of them are beginning to wonder whether his
unexceptionable tenets have any bearing on their working
conditions in this day and age. For the dominant feature
of the present world situation is that until the menace of
mutual nuclear annihilation stared the two main power
blocs in the face, neither side was willing to concede that
there was as much as one single interest that could be
harmonized between them.

Methods, too, have changed. At the Congress of Vienna after the Napoleonic Wars, diplomatic negotiation was still the preserve of aristocrats, of dukes, princes, barons and counts. They all had the same background, spoke the same language and shared the same tastes and manners, no matter what sovereign they represented. Like boys who had been to the same school or college, they knew and understood one another. They argued, bargained and intrigued without banging the table. They swapped towns, provinces, gossip and mistresses without raising their voices. It was all very gentlemanly, polite, civilized, exclusive and secret. The common people played no part in the proceedings, except to gape at their magnificent coaches as they drove from one palace to another in an endless round of conferences, banquets and balls.

Today the form is rather different. To begin with, courteous language is no longer considered essential. Immediately after the Second World War, the epithets that were bandied around were fairly innocuous. Soviet representatives confined themselves to calling the American, British and French governments "imperialist aggressors, capitalist oppressors and warmongers." But when that failed to shake the occupants of the White House, No. 10 Downing Street and the Quai d'Orsay, the animal kingdom was brought in to give the conventional phraseology of Marxist dialectic deeper meaning, and the Western leaders found themselves branded as "ravenous beasts."

It was a line of disputation which reached its climax when the late Andrei Vyshinsky, who had been Stalin's prosecutor at the treason trials in the nineteen-thirties, was sent to the United Nations as chief Soviet delegate. In the space of a single speech he managed to spell out what "beasts" meant: lice, wolves, rats, reptiles, dogs, vultures, snakes and hyenas. The trouble from Vyshinsky's point of view was that he had fired off the lot in one go. He had no reserves left, and so he had to trot out the same menagerie of animals time and time again, which robbed his speeches of their freshness.

At the suggestion of Sir Anthony Eden, who returned as British Foreign Secretary in 1951 after the defeat of the Labor Party, animal names were banished from diplomatic negotiations, and the world settled down to the by then almost sedate name-calling of the pre-Vyshinksy period.

Another aspect of the new style of negotiation to which a diplomat nowadays has to accustom himself is that he can never tell in what setting he may have to do business. He must be prepared for the unexpected. Old, established routines and familiar conventions can no longer be relied upon, for many rulers of the post-war era refuse to play by the book.

Take the case of Dr. Mossadeq of Persia, for instance. There was nothing startling in his policy as such. All he did was to grab the Abadan refinery belonging to the Anglo-Iranian Petroleum Company. Grabbing other people's property has been a favorite pastime in international affairs for centuries, and there were well-settled diplomatic rules for coping with such a situation. The first one laid it down that the ambassador of the injured country had to deliver a strong, stiff note of protest. This is exactly what the British ambassador in Teheran did. But imagine his consternation when, instead of being received in a large,

115

imposing office—the usual setting for this kind of scene—
he was ushered into the presence of an ailing old gentleman
resting on a hospital bed. This was definitely not in the
book of rules.

He would have been less than human if he had not
inquired after the Persian Prime Minister's health. Of
course he was at a disadvantage immediately, and after
that his stern, cold warnings lost much of their icy impact.
It was even more disconcerting for the ambassador when,
at the end of the interview, he saw Dr. Massadeq served
with a whole roast chicken, which was pounced on and
devoured with obvious relish.

The members of the American diplomatic mission which
was dispatched from Washington to mediate in the dispute
found their experience equally confusing. Naturally they
expected Dr. Mossadeq to be strongly anti-British, and
they were not disappointed. With tears streaming down
his lined face, the Doctor denounced the British as
"brigands, exploiters, blackguards." "You Americans,"
he concluded, "just don't know what they are really like,
because to you they are always on their best behavior."

Suddenly there was a knock at the door. A servant came
in with a letter addressed to the Persian Prime Minister.
Dr. Mossadeq excused himself. As he tore open the
envelope and started reading, the flood of tears stopped
abruptly. Walking up and down the room, his face creased
in smiles, he gurgled happily. "It's from my favorite grandson," he explained. "He is doing well at school and
obviously having a very good time."

"And where is your grandson at school?" one of the
Americans inquired politely.

116

"At a famous preparatory school near London," the proud grandfather replied. "I want him to grow up to be like an English gentleman."

After weeks of vainly trying to evolve acceptable formulae of mediation, the Americans eventually became so frustrated that one of them asked a Persian politician how he and his people could put up with Dr. Mossadeq's mixture of tears and fainting fits day after day. The Persian looked hurt and puzzled.

"Naturally everyone in our Parliament, Government and Opposition alike, knows he is acting," he said. "And Dr. Mossadeq knows we know. But as a performance, it is magnificent. You cannot help admiring it, just as you could not help admiring Churchill's performance in the British Parliament in 1940."

The Doctor's erratic ways defeated most of the emissaries sent from London and Washington. Only the late Richard Stokes, who was then Lord Privy Seal in the Labor Government, managed to make some small headway, and his tactics could hardly be called orthodox.

When he arrived in Teheran, Dr. Mossadeq—as was his custom—received him with obvious ill-humor, and interrupted almost as soon as his visitor began explaining his mission.

"You are a Roman Catholic," he said, "and so our negotiations are bound to fail."

The Lord Privy Seal was taken aback for a brief moment. Then he replied stiffly, "My religion has got nothing to do with it."

"Oh, yes it has," the Doctor persisted. "You Roman Catholics don't allow divorce. But according to Moham-

117

medan law, all a man has to do is to say 'I divorce thee' three times, and that's the end of the matter. And Persia has said 'I divorce thee' to Anglo-Iranian. But as a Catholic you wouldn't understand."

The Lord Privy Seal shook his head. "You misread the situation," he said. "This is not a question of divorce but of alimony."

Dr. Mossadeq rocked with laughter. "Good. Very good." And some semblance of negotiations at last got under way.

The most original diplomatic negotiator of the postwar period, however, is undoubtedly Mr. Krushchev. Stalin left his apartments in the Kremlin only seldom. Krushchev, by contrast, always seems to be out and about. When he wants to let the world know what he feels about things, he simply turns up at a diplomatic reception, grabs a glass and starts proposing toasts.

One of the first Western representatives in Moscow to be exposed to this technique was a British diplomat, just before the Soviet leader's visit to Britain in the spring of 1956. Mr. Krushchev opened the bowling by informing him that he thought of traveling to Britain in a Soviet cruiser.

The diplomat made some noncommittal comment, but Mr. Krushchev had already moved on to another topic. Russia and Britain, he recalled mischievously, had had their little wars in the past, and Russian ports, particularly Sebastopol, had known bombardments by British warships. "But," he added, "we are more interested in growing maize."

Before the diplomat could make an appropriate reply,

118

Mr. Krushchev had raised his glass. "Nevertheless, let us drink a toast to the Royal Navy. *Vashe zdorovye* [Good Health]!"

The toast over, Mr. Krushchev returned to the subject of maize-growing. "Unfortunately, NATO does not grow maize, and so we are obliged to pay attention to our armed forces. Nevertheless, let us drink a toast to maize. *Vashe zdorovye!*"

Two years later, he felt sufficiently confident of his technique to take on more than one diplomat at a time. "Listen, you NATO ambassadors," he called out at a party (there were more than a dozen ambassadors present), "now is a good time to talk about agreement. Let us drink a toast to agreement. *Vashe zdorovye! Do Dna* [Bottoms up]!"

No sooner had the glasses been recharged than Mr. Krushchev continued. "We want to be friends with you. Let us drink to friendship. *Do Dna!*"

One of the ambassadors commented that countries outside the Soviet bloc feared Russia. Mr. Krushchev shrugged his shoulders. "We have all we want. We do not want to take anything from anybody. All we wish is peace. To peace! *Do Dna!*"

The ambassador pursued his point, an argument developed, and eventually Mr. Mikoyan stepped in and said to the Soviet leader, "I am sure you have convinced the Ambassador, but his government won't let him agree with us." And Mr. Krushchev was free to propose another toast.

He is, in fact, a great man for parties. On one occasion, when the band broke into a Caucasian "Lezghinka," he pushed Mikoyan and President Brezhnev on to the dance floor and, pointing to Mikoyan, announced proudly, "He's a good dancer. That's why we keep him in his job."

At a reception for President Sukarno of Indonesia, the orchestra slid into a piece called, "Indonesia is free—cha, cha, cha." Mr. Krushchev seized a bongo drum, and after he got tired of beating out the rhythm on it, he picked up Sukarno's silver-knobbed marshal's baton and took over as band leader. President Sukarno promptly suggested that this called for more Soviet credits, but all the change he got out of Krushchev was the anguished cry, "Look. He robs me of everything."

Mr. Krushchev is always ready with the merry, offhand, tongue-in-cheek quip. When President Kennedy told him at their Vienna meeting in 1961 that his wife thought Gromyko had a nice face, he expressed surprise and commented that there were some who said he looked like Nixon.

When Mr. Macmillan, on his visit to the Soviet Union, asked him if his recent speech full of ominous threats on Berlin represented the official attitude of his government, he pointed out mildly that the speech had been made at an election meeting in a constituency near Moscow and that as democratic leaders they both surely knew that one was apt to get carried away a little in the heat of a tensely fought election battle.

And to vary the diet, there is usually a proverb or saying from someone's folklore to hand. Russia, he proclaimed on one occasion, will abandon Communism "when the shrimp learns to whistle." A questioner whom he thought hostile was told, "A dog barks, and the wind carries the sound away." On the theme of capitalist and Communist coexistence, he once remarked, "You cannot force the buffalo to eat meat. The tiger cannot be made to eat grass." Refusing to let inspection teams into the Soviet Union to check on nuclear disarmament, he explained, "We don't want people walking into our bedrooms." And at one large diplomatic reception he announced gravely, "There are ambassadors here who would like to spit on Communism. But don't let us see who can spit farthest, like camels in a rage. We have to maintain minimum sanitary conditions."

Mr. Krushchev has stated repeatedly that he is no diplomat, but he has become the main tourist attraction in Moscow. No less a showman than the late Mike Todd, after watching one of his performances, was overcome with admiration and called him the perfect ad lib man, the world's greatest showman.

Certainly he has made life for foreign diplomats in Moscow more interesting and amusing, but their colleagues who have to do business with his representatives at various conference tables around the world still find the going pretty tough.

On disarmament, for instance, negotiations have been started, abandoned and restarted any number of times since 1945, and their pattern has always been the same. After an imposing opening ceremony, at which the chief Soviet delegate would voice the loftiest principles in the most general terms, the Russians would, once public interest had moved to some other event, put forward a plan which they knew to be completely unacceptable to the West. They would then leave it to the West to keep the negotiations going by putting up a series of counterplans.

121

Usually the Russians would not reject those out of hand, at least to begin with. Indeed, they would never address themselves to a plan as a whole. They would take one aspect out of it, discuss and debate the point for weeks and months, and then, quite suddenly, leave the whole matter hanging in the air, ignore the fact that no conclusion had been reached, and move on to another point, frequently to repeat the same process. This would go on until the moment when, often after years of patient negotiation, there would seem to be a prospect of an agreement some-where on the horizon and a likelihood that the Soviet Union would have to commit itself in detail on a system of effective controls.

At that moment, the Soviet delegates would either walk out of the negotiations, accusing the other side of bad faith, or would demand that the negotiations should con-tinue in Geneva instead of London or New York, or vice versa, or would suggest that the negotiations would have to begin again in another body with a larger or smaller membership.

Even conferences that begin under the most auspicious circumstances eventually become bogged down in some mysterious way and just go on and on. An American diplo-mat experienced in Russian ways, who was loaned to the Geneva Test Ban Conference in 1958 on the assumption that he would be needed only for four or five weeks at the outside, found time to marry his secretary and set up housekeeping. A member of the British delegation who was attached to the Conference on similar terms went two better: he not only married, but had two children.

Yet there appears to have been a subtle change of

atmosphere within these few trying years, not in the negotiations themselves but in the personal relationships outside office hours with the Soviet diplomats and their families. Wives now exchange visits and recipes, husbands meet for an occasional drink off duty, and the children of the Russian delegates play cowboys and Indians in blue jeans.

Even in the conference chamber the Russians, though as unyielding as ever, seem a little less inclined to expend as much wordage in saying "no" as they did a few years ago and instead occasionally give a short, even humorous, answer.

At a meeting some time ago, Lord Home, the British Foreign Secretary, pointed out to Mr. Gromyko that some sort of control system was really necessary, because if there was a suspicious noise coming from Russia, the West had every right to know whether it was a nuclear explosion or just Mr. Molotov falling down the stairs. Mr. Gromyko, with a hint of a faint smile, replied briefly, "That question would not arise. There is no longer any fissionable material left in Mr. Molotov."

Nothing like it would have happened a few years ago. It may have been a little hard on poor old "Auntie Moll," who had fallen from favor long before, but as far as things to come are concerned, it may be a straw in the wind.

11:

The
Not-So-Gentle Art
of Spying

AT SIX O'CLOCK ON THE MORNING OF OCTOBER 15, 1917, the legendary Mata Hari whose sinuous Indian temple dances had won her acclaim in Paris, Berlin, Rome and London, faced a firing squad in the fortress of Vincennes just outside of Paris. A French court martial had found her guilty of espionage. For the previous three years she had lavishly entertained Allied ministers and diplomats. Her lovers had included young officers on a few hours' leave from the front, who in her arms had for a short while forgotten the horror of the slaughter and filth of the trenches.

It is doubtful that any of the odd bits of information which she had gleaned in this way ever proved of any particular value to the German war effort, but once she had been discovered, the traditional price had to be exacted. She paid it gallantly, almost gaily. She refused to be pinioned to the stake in front of the firing squad, or to be blindfolded, and her last act before the officer gave the order to fire was to blow a kiss of farewell to her defense lawyer and the priest who had come to comfort her.

The dangers involved in spying, the penalties for failure, and the ruthlessness, are as harsh today as they were then, but the atmosphere of romance and glamor, of caviar and champagne, is much less in evidence. Igor Gouzenko, the cipher clerk at the Soviet Embassy in Ottawa whose defection in 1945 gave the Western Powers the first inkling of the existence of a vast Soviet spy network in their midst, was a solid family man, living in a modest, middle-class apartment block, and his main concern, once he had made his momentous decision to go over to the West, was not money and a life of ease in return for his information but protection for his wife and small child against Soviet vengeance. To his horror, he found that neither the Canadian Ministry of Justice nor the *Ottawa Journal* paid very much attention to his story, supported though it was by authentic Soviet documents. It was only when Soviet strong-arm men broke into his apartment that he at last received help; and then his rescuers were not the resourceful agents of some Western counterespionage service but his neighbors, ordinary family men like himself. They did not take kindly to the idea of anyone's being pushed around in his own home, and called in the police.

Again, when Vladimir Petrov, a high Soviet Secret Police official attached to the Russian embassy in Canberra, asked for political asylum in Australia in 1954, the central figure in the drama was not a glamorous demimondaine but Mrs. Petrov, a homely, plump, middle-aged Russian housewife. The moment his defection became known, the Russians made her a prisoner in their embassy, intending to use her as a hostage in order to induce her husband to return to the Soviet Union, or at least to keep him from telling the West what he knew. In due course, she was marched to a plane, a distraught, confused figure surrounded by armed Soviet guards, to be flown back to Russia. Only at Darwin, the plane's last stop on Australian soil, was she forcibly separated from her escorts and at last given the opportunity of stating unequivocally that she wanted to stay with her husband.

Gone, in short, are the days of the beautiful spy who bewitches a young diplomat or staff officer of another power and makes off with his country's secrets conveniently condensed on one sheet of paper that can be tucked into the top of her stocking. In our modern, complex, highly industrialized societies, it takes thousands of scraps of information, painstakingly collected by scores of agents day after day, to build up a picture of a rival's intentions, plans and strength. Not that female charm does not still play its part in this new scheme of things, but it is apt to be used with rather less panache and more sordid calculation than in Mata Hari's day. Some time ago a middle-aged American clerk at the United States Embassy in Warsaw became involved in an affair with a young Polish girl who had asked him for food and cigarettes to help her allegedly almost destitute family. One day the Polish secret police surprised him with the girl in a hotel bedroom and took photographs. Being a married man, he allowed himself to be blackmailed into cooperating with the police at least for a short time. He never saw the girl again. She was merely a small functionary in a big intelligence apparatus who dropped out of the picture the moment she had completed her allotted task.

Intelligence work today, in fact, has been taken over by the organization men. The day is past for the brilliant lone operator who goes off, on his own, to ferret out a vital piece of information by a series of schemes he makes up on the spur of the moment, eluding all the traps of the other side's counterespionage service to report back to his own government in person. He exists only in fiction.

In real life, information is obtained in small and often disjointed fragments by agents who have been planted in the other side's territory years before, and from them it is passed back to base along a chain of communication consisting of literally dozens of couriers. In the case of Dr. Fuchs, the atom spy, some couriers held the information they were given for only a few minutes before passing it on to the next link. They had no idea of its nature or, in a few instances, of the kind of work for which they were being used. As a result, the Western counterespionage services took years to uncover the enormous Soviet atomic spy network, even after Dr. Fuchs, Harry Gold and the Rosenbergs had been found out, for in each instance only a few links in the chain were exposed and then, abruptly, the trail grew cold again.

Needless to say, in these circumstances, the present-day "spy-master" tends to regard the lone wolf as nothing but a nuisance. Moreover, modern science has made many of the individual exploits of former days unnecessary. When Britain in the last century wanted details of a fortress on the Dalmatian coast, Baden-Powell, who later founded the Boy Scout movement, succeeded in getting close enough to sketch its guns and fortifications by disguising himself as a somewhat scatterbrained and bibulous entomologist in search of a rare species of butterfly. Similar information today can be obtained more quickly, more fully and more accurately by a fast high-altitude plane equipped with cameras and radar. In 1943 it was not a spy ring operating inside Nazi Germany which discovered that Hitler's scientists were on the point of perfecting an unmanned flying bomb but a young officer in the Women's Royal Air Force working in an R.A.F. headquarters in England. During a routine examination of aerial reconnaissance photographs taken over Germany the previous day she came across a picture of Peenemunde, the German rockets research and guided missiles station on the Baltic. Scrutinizing it with a stereoscope and a measuring magnifier, she discovered a small curving shadow, and above it, a T-shaped white blob which she eventually decided might be a kind of launching ramp with a small airplane on it. The picture was enlarged, and the experts confirmed her suspicions. As a result of her discovery Peenemunde became one of the R.A.F.'s main targets; production of the V1's was delayed by almost a year; and although London suffered considerable damage when the "doodle-bugs" were eventually unloosed in 1944, their production was never large enough to enable Hitler to launch his planned full-scale bombardment of the whole of Southern England and thus prevent the Allied build-up for D-day and the liberation of Europe.

Equally valuable technical aids to intelligence, particularly Western intelligence, are the finely tuned receiving instruments which enable skilled operators to listen in to domestic broadcasts in Russia, China and other dictatorships. The radio, after all, is the most important communications link between rulers and ruled in "closed" societies. It is the instrument by which dictatorial governments seek to mold public opinion and shape views, and what they say and how they talk to their people can give important clues to their plans and policies.

In the summer of 1958, when the revolution in Iraq and the assassination of King Feisal threatened to plunge the whole Middle East into chaos, and the United States and Britain moved troops into the Lebanon and Jordan to stabilize the situation, Krushchev fired off a series of angry notes warning the Western powers that their action had pushed the world to the brink of war. Washington and London remained unperturbed—to the consternation of many observers, who regarded their attitude as reckless brinkmanship. The two governments, however, had good reason for their seemingly unnatural calmness. At the height of the Middle East crisis, the West's radio eavesdroppers reported that Krushchev had left Moscow for a speech-making tour of Central Russia. His subject: "How to Grow more Corn." On Russian domestic stations, events in the Middle East were dismissed in a sentence or two. Since no attempt was made to prepare the Russian people psychologically for a possible major test of strength in that area, it was obvious that Krushchev was merely using one of his favorite weapons—bluff.

A little later, John Foster Dulles, who was then Secre-

tary of State, unexpectedly issued a blunt warning to the
Soviet Union that Washington would treat the slightest
encroachment on Turkish soil as an attack on the United
States. To many his statement seemed like deliberate prov-
ocation. After all, under the North Atlantic Alliance every
NATO country, including the United States, was bound
automatically to come to Turkey's aid if she were attacked;
so why make a point of spelling out America's commit-
ment in respect of one specific member country at this
particular juncture? What was not generally known was
that a report of some local festivities, broadcast by a South
Russian station, mentioned Marshal Rokossovsky as one
of the guests and described him as "the new commander-
in-chief of the Transcaucasian military region."

The disturbing feature of the report was that the Transcaucasian command stretches right down to the Turkish
province of Anatolia, to which Russia has always laid
claim, and that in ordinary times it would be considered
far too junior a post for someone of the seniority of Marshal Rokossovsky, a master of attack and one of the most
brilliant Soviet commanders in the Second World War.
There were only two possible explanations: either Rokossovsky had fallen from favor or the Soviet Union intended
to seize Anatolia in one fell swoop and then leave the West
with the awkward choice of accepting a fait accompli or
risking nuclear war over a piece of territory of which few
people in America or Western Europe had ever heard. The
State Department decided to take no chances. Dulles'
abrupt warning was meant to serve notice on the Soviet
Union that however occupied the United States might be
in other parts of the world, Washington was keeping a

close watch on developments on the Soviet-Turkish border. Marshal Rokossovsky was moved from the Transcaucasian command shortly afterwards.

Intelligence information has been essential to policy-making through the ages, for as Sun Tsu, who analyzed political and military events in China five centuries before Christ, pointed out in one of his books, "What enables the wise sovereign and the good general to strike and conquer, and achieve things beyond the reach of ordinary men, is foreknowledge." To be capable of providing that fore-knowledge, intelligence services have always been exempted from having to conform to the ordinary rules of decent conduct. Their agents can play truant from the moral and religious obligations that bind other men. They can cheat, lie, steal, maim and even kill.

Indeed, there is only one crime, as far as an agent is concerned—to be found out. And if he is guilty of that, his government will disown him instantly without batting an eyelid. His discovery will certainly not be allowed to cloud ordinary diplomatic relations for long. Of course, the government whose counterespionage service captured the agent may fire off a strongly worded protest couched in terms of outraged innocence, but it knows its note will be rejected. The agent's government will blandly disregard any evidence linking it with the agent and disclaim all knowledge of him and his activities. The whole procedure has been hallowed by long usage, and so long as everyone plays this rather cynical charade according to the rules, there need be no unnecessary or lasting awkwardness.

The only statesman who has ever flouted the rules was President Eisenhower in 1960 when he publicly accepted personal responsibility for the flight of the U2 reconnaissance plane which came down some one thousand five hundred miles inside the Soviet Union. The consequences were far from happy, although the sensational collapse of the Big Four summit meeting in Paris shortly afterwards was not one of them. Admittedly, Krushchev branded Eisenhower an "aggressor" and "warmonger" and refused in his loudest table-thumping style to have anything to do with him, but he is too tough and shrewd a character to wreck a diplomatic occasion from which he hopes to derive some benefit merely for the sake of exploiting the other side's embarrassment over the mishandling of an intelligence operation.

When, a few years earlier, during his visit to England, British naval intelligence had been caught trying to take a look at the underwater defenses of the Soviet cruiser which had brought him to Portsmouth, there were no tantrums, no outbursts. His temper remained calm and sweet, and the only reference he allowed himself to make about the affair was good-humored. "Much to the disgust of my admirals," he told an audience of British businessmen, "cruisers have lost all value in modern war. The only purpose they can still usefully be made to serve is to take people like myself on ceremonial visits. But they're expensive to keep just for that alone." The reason for his restraint was very simple: his visit to Britain was the first he was making to a Western country, and he was determined that it should be a success. Nothing was to be allowed to mar it.

In the case of the Paris summit meeting, however, his attitude was very different. He was at the time having trouble with his die-hard Stalinists at home, who suspected him of being "soft" in his dealings with the West. Consequently, he had little or no room for maneuvering on any of the topics like Berlin, Germany, disarmament or nuclear tests, which de Gaulle, Macmillan and Eisenhower wanted to discuss with him, and he knew that he was in danger of appearing in the world's opinion unhelpful, if not downright obstructionist. It was not a prospect he relished, and Eisenhower's personal assumption of responsibility for the U2 flight provided him with a highly welcome excuse for wrecking the meeting before it could get down to matters of substance. But if he had not had that excuse, he would have had to find another. The Paris meeting was doomed in any case.

What was not doomed, until the President accepted responsibility for the U2 flight, was the visit he was to pay to the Soviet Union later that year at Krushchev's invitation. Arrangements for his trip were well advanced, with tours to Leningrad and Kiev and a series of public speeches and appearances planned for Soviet television. Eisenhower himself attached great importance to his visit, and certainly no American was better fitted than he, with his unique gift of radiating warmth and understanding to vast crowds, to jolly and smile ordinary Russians out of the preconceived notion they had instilled in them of America's rulers as calculating, blood-thirsty, money-grabbing imperialists. After all, in 1950, when he returned to Europe as the first Supreme Commander of the newly formed NATO forces, the Communist attempt to paint him as a scheming warmonger had collapsed rapidly because no one, not even Party faithfuls, had found the label convincing.

The President's acceptance of direct responsibility for an act which was admitted to be contrary to international law made the cancellation of the Soviet invitation inevitable. In the circumstances, the Chairman of the Soviet Council of Ministers could no more receive him than the President could have received Krushchev in the previous year if the Russian leader had made himself personally and publicly responsible for any of the Soviet agents convicted of spying in the United States.

When the chairman of the Senate Foreign Relations Committee, Senator Fulbright, asked Secretary of State Herter in the course of hearings following the U2 incident whether he thought that anything had been learned from the affair, the Secretary of State smiled wryly and replied, "Not to have accidents." He might have added, "And if there are accidents, not to link the Administration with them."

Certainly statesmen and diplomats are well-advised to keep the grim, gray, twilight world of intelligence work at a distance, especially nowadays when the growing volume of intelligence activity at so many levels of society in so many different countries inevitably increases the danger of mishaps.

Before the Second World War, America's intelligence services were, to put it mildly, rudimentary. The country was determined to stay aloof from other nations' quarrels; so why bother to spend a lot of time and money to collect information about faraway people and places which Washington's policy-makers and military planners were never likely to need? Of course there was the F.B.I. to track down foreign agents inside the country, and the Army and Navy tried with the limited resources at their disposal to follow what other countries' armies and navies were up to, while the State Department kept an eye on political trends abroad. But when one Captain Dean Rusk, later to become President Kennedy's Secretary of State, was ordered to Washington after Pearl Harbor to take over the "British Empire" section of G2 (military intelligence), the section responsible for providing the War Department's planners with the political, economic, geographical and military information on all the places in the British Empire where American forces were about to go into action, he found that the sum total of his files consisted of a handful of yellowing *New York Times* clippings, a handbook on India and Ceylon and a military attaché's report filed from London in 1925. He discovered that the knowledge about Britain and the British Empire which he carried in his head as a result of his days as a Rhodes scholar at Oxford was more extensive and up-to-date.

Today the United States, with its world-wide commitments, boasts more than a dozen intelligence services, of which the most important is the Central Intelligence Agency. Established in 1947 to correlate and evaluate data gathered by its own agents and those of the other services and to provide the National Security Council with intelligence information on matters of high policy, the C.I.A. headquarters staff of more than ten thousand is housed in an imposing eight-story building near Langley, Virginia, on a site that covers one hundred and forty acres.

The C.I.A. is also charged by Congress to engage in

and perform such "additional services" as the National Security Council might require, meaning espionage and sabotage. Its budget, which is never published, has been estimated to lie somewhere between five hundred and eight hundred million and its director who, apart from the headquarters personnel, controls thousands of agents all over the world, is the only United States Government agency head who can personally authorize the spending of millions of dollars of his organization's budget with no public questions asked.

Britain's intelligence services are more compact, and because of their smaller size, less bureaucratically organized, but the profusion of different intelligence services is quite as bewildering as in the United States. Military Intelligence is made up of about a dozen branches—their exact number varies—of which the most famous is M15, a counterintelligence service which always has a civilian head who works closely with Scotland Yard's Special Branch. Needless to say, the Foreign Office dabbles in intelligence, as does the Board of Trade. The Ministry of Defence has the Joint Intelligence Bureau which concentrates on coordination, analysis and evaluation, and both the Royal Navy and the Royal Air Force operate intelligence divisions in Britain and abroad. But to most people the administrative divisions between the various organizations are obscure and irrelevant. They lump the lot together in one package: the British Secret Service.

Few bodies engaged in intelligence work have ever enjoyed so great a reputation for omniscience and omnipotence on so little hard and solid evidence of achievement. As soon as there is unrest in the Middle East or an uprising somewhere in Asia, someone will sooner or later claim to detect the hidden hand of the Secret Service. An official denial from London will merely produce knowing nods in the bazaars. Silence will have the same result. The Secret Service cannot lose.

Admittedly, at the time of Suez, in 1956, the Secret Service's reputation took somewhat of a knock; but such is the strength of the legend that tales of its resourcefulness and infinite cunning circulate today as freely as ever. Books like Graham Greene's *Our Man in Havana,* which seek to debunk it, serve only to enhance its fame. It is indestructible, and the unspoken thought in most people's minds seems to be that it is bound to come out on top in the end. The lesson appears to be this: If you have a Secret Service—and most particularly if you have not—keep it secret.

By far the most formidable and sinister intelligence "Apparat" in Western eyes at the moment is that of the Soviet Union. From its headquarters in the Kremlin, known as the "Center," its tentacles reach out into the farthest corners of the earth, undermining, corrupting and forever sucking up information like some giant invisible octopus. It appears to be everywhere. There seems to be no place it cannot penetrate, no secret it cannot ferret out, no country where it cannot count on the help and support of local Communist sympathizers. In short, it seems the perfect instrument for undercover intelligence work—until one looks at some of the stories brought to light during the postwar spy trials in the United States and Britain and at the hearings of the Royal Commissions in Canada and Australia after Gouzenko's and Petrov's defections. Ineptness, one discovers, is not a prerogative of Western intelligence. Certainly the evidence suggests that working for the mysterious and allegedly all-powerful Soviet Secret Service is about as exciting as clerking in an insurance office.

Take for instance, the case of the young Soviet agent who struck up an acquaintance with a good-looking lady cipher clerk at a French embassy in the Pacific. Here, on the face of it, were all the ingredients of a classic spy story: love, intrigue and treachery—a fascinating mixture of affairs of State and of the heart. The two met secretly from time to time in some secluded park or out-of-the-way restaurant, and after a few weeks the Soviet agent was able to report to headquarters in Moscow that the lady's attachment to him was "deepening." Moscow was full of praise.

It was at this point, however, that the story departed from the traditional pattern. The agent felt that if he was to further his cause, the time had come to present the lady with a token of his affection, and he decided on a watch. Now you might have thought that any self-respecting Secret Service man would have enough funds at his disposal for just such a contingency, but this apparently is not so in the Soviet Secret Service. Every form of expenditure has to be authorized by Moscow, and when our agent applied for authorization, Moscow's first reaction was, Why? Hasn't she got a watch already? In a series of lengthy communications, which of course he had to put laboriously into code, the agent tried to explain the psychology of courtship in the capitalist world to his bosses in Moscow. It was over a month before they eventually gave their grudging approval. But by this time it was too late. The psychological moment had passed, and a promising romance had withered and died.

The meanness of the Soviet Secret Service seems to know no limits, but Moscow's economy drives have not always had the desired results. Some years ago head-quarters objected to the amount of money one of their agents in Sydney, Australia, was spending on taxis. It would be cheaper, they claimed, if they bought him a car and put him on a mileage allowance.

A car was duly bought. The only trouble was that he couldn't pass his driving test. Moscow authorized funds for driving lessons, and then more funds, but all to no purpose. The poor man failed his test time and again. In the end, he applied for transfer to another post. He was willing, he explained in desperation, to be dropped by parachute anywhere in the capitalist world to do subversive work, but he just could not face the Sydney traffic.

The "Center" in Moscow plainly dislikes being drawn into ideological arguments, particularly about Marxism, but when one of its agents in Canberra, Australia, made contact with a cipher clerk at a Western embassy who wanted to know more about the Marxist interpretation of contemporary history, it decided to make an exception. After all, cipher clerks in the other side's camp are valu-able acquisitions for any intelligence service, and so the "Center" patiently fed its agent, whose Marxism must have been very rusty, with answers to the many queries raised by the clerk. All went well until the agent asked to be briefed on the background to the 1939 Nazi-Soviet pact, the most sensational reversal of Soviet policy in recent history, which virtually gave Hitler carte blanche to do what he liked in Europe. It rocked the Communist movement to its foundation at the time and is still not one of the favorite topics of conversation among Party members.

In this instance the "Center" refused to play. Has the time not come, it pointedly asked its agent, to talk a little more about codes and a little less about ideology?

The most unpleasant aspect of the Soviet Secret Service has always been, and still is, the way in which it uses relatives to bring pressure on its agents. But even there, mistakes have been known to occur. When Moscow got wind of the fact that one of its agents might be about to go over to the other side, it promptly checked what members of his family were still in the Soviet Union. To their horror they found no one except his mother-in-law. In a desperate attempt to bring him to heel, she was made to write to her son-in-law. But her letter had no effect. He replied with a flourish that he had chosen freedom.

In theory, of course, Soviet agents in the West have one great advantage: they operate in "open" societies. They can buy detailed maps of every region; they can glean exact data about steel and coal production from the newspapers; they can find out what military planes the United States or Britain are building by following the debates in Congress or Parliament; and they can collect substantial dossiers on most politicians, diplomats, generals, industrialists and trade union leaders from newspaper clippings.

But in practice it is doubtful if they make the best of their advantage. Like most Nazi agents before the Second World War, many of them seem to spend a great deal of time, energy and money in seeking out information they could easily look up in any public library. How else can

141

one explain the curious fact that quite a few Soviet agents continue to be caught in suspicious circumstances near dock areas when the Chambers of Commerce of most ports are only too eager to advertise the amount of tonnage that can be handled, and the available storage and transport facilities.

Naturally, no agent who takes a pride in his work likes to have things made too easy. It must be galling to be instructed to report on the command structure of the American armed forces and then to discover that there is a Pentagon handout on the subject which is available to the public and constantly kept up to date. Suspicious by nature and devious by training, agents tend to reject the obvious, to prefer the involved and circuitous. An "open" society that carelessly thrusts its vital statistics under their noses can in its way be as confusing and perplexing as a "closed" society. Despite all the publicly available information on America's industrial resources, Nazi Germany failed to appreciate how rapidly United States production could be made to expand.

Western intelligence, for its part, tends to be less handicapped today by Russia's "closed" society than it was ten or fifteen years ago. The growing numbers of scientists, technologists and engineers need magazines and journals to keep themselves informed of trends and developments in their various fields. The spread of education compels the newspapers to fill their space with less propaganda and more reports of what is actually happening. The reports may still be slanted, or downright falsehoods, but to the trained observer, the expert Sovietologist or Kremlinologist, they provide valuable clues. Above all, the

Soviet Union's leaders no longer live in splendid isolation in the seclusion of the Kremlin. They feel they have to be out and about, expounding their policies, explaining away failures, encouraging, and if possible, persuading. Stalin emerged at only infrequent intervals to lay down the Party line in one of his rare five- or six-hour speeches, and for months—and sometimes years—afterwards Soviet-ologists had to be content to mine his turgid, cryptic and virtually indigestible prose in the hope of extracting a few nuggets of information and future intentions. Krushchev, by comparison, never stops talking, and many Sovietologists who once complained bitterly that there was too little to work on are now in despair because there is too much. It is estimated that as much as seventy-five percent of all the information on the Soviet Union nowadays comes from open and not secret sources.

Of course it still takes a mind with a knowledge of Communist ideology and an intuitive understanding of Marxist thought processes to make anything of the available information. In 1953, shortly after Stalin's death, when the Soviet Union was run by a triumvirate consisting of Malenkov, Molotov and Beria, Moscow Radio was overheard broadcasting an announcement that a Professor Meir Vovsi had received a decoration for his services to Soviet medicine. It seemed a trivial item. But for the Soviet expert to whom it was reported, the name rang a bell, and he consulted his files. Vovsi, he found was one of the "terrorist physicians" who, just before Stalin's death, had been imprisoned for "prescribing harmful treatment with a view to cutting short the lives of Soviet leaders." The expert knew from experience that if a man like Vovsi was suddenly rehabilitated, it was time for whoever was responsible for locking him up to look out; and since the person responsible was Beria, the Minister of State Security and a member of the ruling triumvirate, he concluded that the struggle for Stalin's succession had been joined and was about to erupt into the open. Shortly afterwards, Beria was arrested and executed.

In the final analysis, the key to success in all intelligence work lies in the interpretation and evaluation of the available raw material. Western intelligence would gain nothing by planting an agent in the Kremlin next to Krushchev, or Soviet intelligence by having an agent sit opposite President Kennedy at the National Security Council, unless their respective reports are assessed objectively and imaginatively. And it is remarkable how many intelligence "coups" have been ruined by faulty evaluation. Even the most brilliant intelligence analysts, it appears, are as apt as ordinary mortals to allow prejudice, moral considerations or a reluctance to change course in the light of fresh evidence to cloud their judgment.

When the American military attaché in Berlin in the late nineteen-thirties reported that Hitler's Wehrmacht had become the strongest military force in Europe, Washington thought he was exaggerating. It could not bring itself to accept that a system which was morally evil could be efficient. For many years after the Second World War, British Intelligence persistently overestimated the strength of the Arabs and underestimated the power of Israel. Before the abortive invasion of Cuba in 1961, the Central Intelligence Agency confidently predicted that practically the whole of Cuba would rise against Castro the moment the landings took place. Evidence to the contrary was dismissed as unreliable or irrelevant.

But the biggest and costliest mistake in evaluation in recent times was made by Stalin. Early in 1941 Soviet agents got wind of Hitler's plan to attack Russia. In due course they even managed to extract the exact date for the invasion, June 22. The Soviet General Staff was convinced the reports were accurate, but Stalin thought otherwise. He suspected the information had been planted to provoke him into mobilizing the Red Army and so antagonizing Hitler, his "nonbelligerent" partner; and to the consternation of his generals he refused to take the most elementary military precautions.

It so happened that British agents in Central Europe and the Balkans were reporting large-scale German troop movements at about the same time. Unlike the Soviet General Staff, however, Britain's top intelligence experts rejected the theory that an attack on Russia was imminent. Why, they argued, should the Wehrmacht take on Russia when its Eastern flank was secured by the Nazi-Soviet pact of "nonbelligerency" and there were much more valuable prizes to be won in the Middle East? It seemed unreasonable. It was a line of argument that did not commend itself to Churchill. He rejected their evaluation and demanded to see all the raw material on which their assessment had been based. As a result, he came to the conclusion that an attack was imminent; and although relations between "nonbelligerent" Moscow and embattled London were strained at the time, the British ambassador was instructed to call on the Soviet government immediately with all the relevant information.

145

Churchill might have saved himself the trouble. His ambassador's démarche merely confirmed Stalin in his suspicion that the whole thing was a deep and devious plot, obviously of British origin, to lure him into trouble.

It was a mistake that was to cost Russia millions of avoidable casualties and almost bring the country to its knees.

12:

How To
Behave As
A Diplomat

ALL OF US PUT A FOOT WRONG SOMETIMES, AND DIPLOMATS
are no exception. The trouble in their case is that their
slightest faux pas is immediately treated as an act of State.

Nobody objects when foreign newspapermen, sent to
cover a Presidential election, allow their preference for
one candidate or the other to color their reporting; but
when, during the campaign of 1888, the British Minister
in Washington, Lord Sackville, wrote a letter which could
be interpreted as favoring the re-election of President
Cleveland, there was a public outcry, and Lord Sackville
was handed his passports. The strongest objections, inci-
dentally, came from President Cleveland, who felt that

147

endorsement by a British diplomat was just about the biggest disaster that could befall a candidate, especially as far as the Irish-American vote was concerned.

Again, Germany's neighbors have by now become reconciled to the fact that a great number of German tourists know no greater joy, when on holiday abroad, than to run down the local cooking, hotel accommodation and sanitary arrangements and to proclaim loudly and frequently how much better things are ordered at home in Germany; but when a few years ago the wife of a West German attaché in London chose to address a few words to the German embassy staff on the subject of correct behavior and asked her listeners not to forget that they were in "enemy territory," everyone agreed that Anglo-German relations would be best served by having the lady return to the Fatherland as quickly as possible.

Obviously, no diplomat can long expect to remain at his post if he gives offense to his hosts, and the surest way of doing so is to interfere in their politics. Queen Elizabeth I sent a number of French and Spanish ambassadors packing when she discovered that they were involved in plots to overthrow and assassinate her. Mr. Morris, the American representative in Paris at the time of the French Revolution, was asked to leave because he had not only objected publicly to the deliberate use of terror by France's new rulers but also because he had played an active part in trying to help Louis XVI and Marie Antoinette escape from Paris. At about the same time the United States Government told the French minister, M. Genest, to go back to his native land on the ground that fitting out French privateers in American ports and then using them to capture British merchant ships, often in American territorial waters, was hardly a diplomatic activity. In 1915 Dr. Dumba, the Austro-Hungarian ambassador in Washington, was sent home for advising Vienna on how to foment strikes in American munitions factories, and so was Captain Franz von Papen, the German military attaché who was suspected of organizing sabotage activities in American ports and industrial plants. Von Papen was to capture international attention some seventeen years later when he helped Hitler to become Chancellor of Germany.

These, of course, are extreme cases. A diplomat who wants to be "handed his passports" or to be told that "he has outlived his usefulness and is no longer considered persona grata" need not go to quite such lengths. In 1898 Senor de Lôme lost his job as Spanish Minister in Washington for calling President McKinley "weak and a bidder for the admiration of the crowd besides being a would-be politician." In 1927 M. Rakovsky, the Soviet ambassador in Paris, had to return to Moscow after calling on French soldiers, in the event of war with Russia, to join the Red Army. In 1952 the Soviet Union insisted on the recall of Mr. George F. Kennan, the United States ambassador in Moscow, because of disparaging remarks he was alleged to have made about Soviet Russia. And in 1955 the West German cultural attaché in Rome found himself very much "non grata" after describing Italy in a Munich beer cellar as "a delightful land of spaghetti and macaroni, with a bishop in every third village, a marked absence of organizing ability and a corrupt administration." For good measure, he concluded by taking a swipe not only at the country to which he was accredited but also at the United

States. According to him the Italians and the Americans had three things in common: they delighted in noise, they spoiled their children stupidly and needlessly, and they put up vast billboards everywhere which ruined the countryside. After that performance, the West German Foreign Ministry had considerable doubts as to whether the attaché could be usefully employed in any post anywhere.

Needless to say, there are also occasions where a diplomat can find himself "non grata" through no fault or indiscretion of his own. Whenever a Soviet or satellite diplomat is caught spying and sent home, Moscow or the satellite Government concerned will, within forty-eight hours, discover evidence of "undiplomatic activity" against a Western diplomat. The curious feature of these incidents is that if the Communist diplomat happens to have been, say, a Second Secretary, then the evidence of "undiplomatic activity" which comes so conveniently to light at just the right moment will incriminate a Second Secretary in a Western embassy—never a First or a Third Secretary. Reciprocity is strictly observed on these occasions.

One of the most delicate problems facing a diplomat is the question of what contact he can permit himself with the political opponents of the government to which he is accredited. In the old days there was no problem, and the answer to the question was simply, none whatever. No king, in times when monarchs were still absolute, wanted to see foreign ambassadors in touch with the factions which made up his court, and in a great many capitals it was even unwise for a diplomat to be observed talking to the crown prince. Kings and their heirs seldom got on well. If the king was reactionary, the crown prince usually liked to give himself progressive airs, and where the heir belonged to the peace party, the king was bound to favor the war faction. Ambassadors therefore were well advised to have dealings only with those who actually wielded power.

It is a rule that still holds good today in dictatorships. Clearly no ambassador should have any contact with underground opposition groups; nor should he allow himself to be dragged into the involved, Byzantine intrigues by which personal and policy differences in a one-party dictatorship are often resolved. His job is first and foremost to convey clearly and concisely the views of his government in Washington, London or Paris to the man or men in power and to see that their reactions are accurately reported back to his home government. The series of secret diplomatic exchanges between Kennedy and Krushchev as a result of which the world was pulled back from the brink of nuclear war at the height of the Cuban crisis in the last week of October, 1962, could never have taken place if Krushchev had been distracted by the suspicion that Foy Kohler, the United States ambassador in Moscow, might be playing a dark, deep game with some potential rival in the Kremlin.

Curiously enough, the rules of conduct for a diplomat are less simple and more blurred in a democracy; and diplomats, especially from countries with autocratic regimes, have occasionally found difficulties in adapting themselves. The Duc d'Aumont was left in no doubt about the position when he was sent to London as French ambassador in 1712. His instructions stated explicitly, "The English Constitution is such that the Court of St.

151

James's is not offended if Ambassadors have relations with the Opposition. The Duc d'Aumont need not, therefore, spurn the society of the Whigs."

Certainly in London today an ambassador can do few things more calculated to harm his reputation than to ignore the Leader of Her Majesty's Loyal Opposition. One astonished ambassador even had the extraordinary experience some years ago of being taken aside by the Prime Minister of the day and told to make a friend of the Opposition leader, whom he would discover to be "not a bad chap." As matters stood, the Prime Minister went on to explain, the ambassador was likely to find himself having to deal with him before very long.

In Washington, life can be more confusing still. There may be no official opposition, but apart from the President and the Secretary of State, there are Senators and Congressmen who have an important say in foreign policy matters. As the representative of one of the smaller powers remarked wearily on a recent occasion, "There are so many people to please—and to offend." Congressional committees have been known to reduce, or even to cut out completely, aid to a particular country; and a President may for a number of reasons not always find the moment opportune to fight for a restoration of the cuts. With this knowledge at the back of his mind, what is a foreign diplomat to do if a Congressman asks him, in the blunt, direct way legislators have, to give him certain information about his country's politics and economics relevant to the proposed aid? If he agrees, will he offend the State Department, which has already been asked for this information? If he refuses, will he make an enemy of the Congressman?

It is a tricky situation, calling for tact and a fine sense of judgment. On the whole, the State Department tends to be tolerant. After all, it is as conscious of the realities of the distribution of power in Washington and as keen to see the President's policies implemented as the diplomat. But it draws the line at positive lobbying and at attempts to thwart the President's policies through Congress. Some years ago, a Latin American diplomat fed the Senate Foreign Affairs Committee with information behind the back of the State Department. He escaped being declared "non grata" only because it became evident that this was the custom in his own country. In the circumstances, it was felt that he should therefore be given a chance to mend his ways. No such leniency was shown to a diplomat who took it upon himself—shortly before a Congressional Committee was to begin hearings on a bill granting aid to neutralist countries—to launch a campaign among carefully selected Congressmen denouncing the wickedness and immorality of such a policy. The State Department did not mind his opposition to the policy; it objected solely to his choice of audience in voicing his opposition. Ambassadors, after all, are accredited to the President and not to Congress, and it was to the White House that he should have brought his objections at the time the policy was formulated, and not to Congress when the bill implementing the policy was in the legislative pipeline.

Every government, of course, wants its diplomats to be regarded as "personae gratae" by the people they must deal with, but it will not take kindly to their becoming too "gratae." Above all, it will soon become suspicious if

153

its representatives are showered with gifts by some foreign government.

In 1793, admittedly, nobody thought it extraordinary that the Russian government, at the conclusion of some trade negotiations with Britain, should make the two undersecretaries at the Foreign Office a present of three hundred pounds each and share out another four hundred pounds among ten Foreign Office clerks. Today no official of the Foreign Office or the State Department could expect to remain in his country's service for long if, at the end of some long-drawn-out negotiations in Geneva, he was found to have received a cash payment from the Soviet Union.

In not every case however, is the position so simple. Kings, presidents and prime ministers often like to express their friendship and appreciation by making what they look upon as little personal presents, and to refuse could give great offence. The problem is where to draw the line. Unfortunately there are no hard and fast rules. It is, according to Mr. John Foster Dulles, "all a question of taste." By that token fountain pens, lighters, silver-framed photographs, jewel-encrusted gold cigarette cases and precious porcelain services seem all right, but a three-thousand-dollar car, which the State Department's assistant chief of protocol accepted from King Saud of Saudi Arabia some years ago, was not.

Governments tend to be equally suspicious of diplomats who accept foreign decorations. Indeed, most of them explicitly forbid the practice for reasons which are probably not very different from those of Elizabeth I. She once explained, "I would not have my sheep branded with any

154

other mark than my own, or follow the whistle of a strange shepherd."

The business of being "persona grata" begins long before a diplomat takes up his post abroad, at least in the case of ambassadors. As soon as a government has decided whom it wants to be represented by in a foreign capital, it submits the name to the foreign government to discover if its choice would be acceptable. If the answer is no, then that is the end of the matter, no matter how preposterous the reason for the rejection may seem.

In 1757 Sweden refused to accept Goodrich as the British envoy because he had visited a country with which Sweden happened to be at war at the time. In 1832 the Czar rejected Sir Stratford Canning as British Ambassador simply because he could not stand the man. In 1847 the king of Hanover, a Protestant, turned down a prospective envoy who was a Roman Catholic. In 1891 China refused to have anything to do with H. W. Blair, a former United States Senator, on the ground that he had "bitterly abused China in the Senate" and "was conspicuous in helping to pass the oppressive Exclusion Act" restricting the number of Chinese who could enter the United States. At about the same time the imperial Court of the Hapsburgs refused to receive one Keiley as United States envoy because he was married to a Jewess and therefore considered socially unacceptable in Vienna according to the rules of etiquette still prevailing there then. The President in Washington made no secret of his strong distaste for Vienna's reasons, but there was nothing he could do to force Keiley's acceptance. He had to content himself with refusing to nominate anyone else as United States envoy, and as a result the

American legation in Vienna was run by a mere secretary for some considerable time.

Similar incidents are unlikely to happen today, largely because few countries can permit themselves the luxury of allowing social prejudices to deprive them of the advantages of proper American diplomatic representation. Nevertheless, to avoid embarrassment and hurt feelings, the preliminary inquiries about an ambassador's suitability are always made as quickly and discreetly as possible. In the case of prospective United States ambassadors, they take place before the nomination is officially announced by the White House and submitted to the Senate for confirmation. If it were otherwise, the possibilities of generating international disharmony would be endless. For one thing, the Senate—or at least some members of it—could not be expected to take kindly to a country which rejected an appointee of whom it had just approved; and for another, Senatorial hearings, with their tendency to drag into public view all the foolish and indiscreet things a nominee may have said in years past, may convince the receiving country that the only course open to it is a declaration of "persona non grata."

Let us assume, however, that our prospective ambassador has cleared all the preliminary hurdles. If he is a non-career diplomat, he will then discover that ambassadors do not start their jobs like ordinary mortals in less lofty walks of life. It's not done to book a seat on the first airplane to the foreign capital. In fact, it's particularly undignified to appear too eager to get down to work. There is a certain stylized, slow-motion pace that must be observed. Several weeks are usually allowed to elapse between the formal announcement of the appointment and the departure. The ambassador-to-be fills his days with a leisurely round of meetings and calls. He consults government officials, is briefed on current problems and attends lunches and dinners given for him by societies with special cultural or economic interests in the country to which he is being sent. Finally, he is summoned to present himself to his Head of State. President Kennedy likes these farewells to take the form of informal chats. In Britain, the Queen makes a point, whenever possible, of having the new ambassador and his wife to lunch at Buckingham Palace. And in Paris, President de Gaulle seldom fails to send away a departing envoy without a stirring message.

In the meantime, the Protocol Department of the Foreign Ministry or State Department is busy drawing up the ambassador's letter of credence or credentials, the document by which his own Head of State accredits him to the Head of State of the country to which he is being sent. The language which protocol lays down for these communications is rigidly formal and politely ignores any differences that may exist between states. President Kennedy, for example, always addresses other Heads of States as "Great and Good Friend," whether the addressee be the Queen of England or President Brezhnev of the Soviet Union. "You only cease being a "Great and Good Friend," protocol experts explain, "when diplomatic relations are broken off or war breaks out."

The formula is varied only if both states involved are monarchies. For instance, when Queen Elizabeth II sends greetings to another crowned head, "Good Friend" becomes "Sir My Brother," irrespective of whether she is

157

addressing the Emperor of Japan or a close relative like the King of Norway.

According to protocol experts, departure from this seemingly absurd phraseology invariably leads to trouble. They recall the occasion in the last century when France almost broke off diplomatic relations with Russia because the Czar had addressed Napoleon III as "Friend" and not as "Brother." Napoleon III, of course, always suspected Europe's other reigning houses of thinking of him as a common upstart, and he was not in the least mollified when the Czar replied to his protest by pointing out that one could choose one's friends but not one's relations.

All letters of credence follow roughly the same pattern, though there are small local variations. The President of the United States always stresses how "well informed of the relative interests of the two countries" the new ambassador is, and pays tribute to "his high character and ability," while in England the Queen writes of the "talents and zeal" of her ambassador, whom she calls "Trusty and Well-Beloved." And when it comes to the gist of the letter —the request to give credence to all the new ambassador says—the respective formulations spotlight the different concepts of sovereignty in the two countries. The Queen demands that the ambassador be heard "in Our name," and the President, "on the part of the United States."

Fully briefed and furnished with all the necessary credentials, the new ambassador may feel that he can at long last get going, but he will find that protocol still frowns on unseemly haste. If he wants to fly, it will be impressed upon him that traveling by liner and train would be much more dignified. And even when he eventually arrives in the foreign capital, he will discover that he has no "formal" existence until after he has presented officially his letter of credence—no simple matter, since the Head of State is the only person entitled to receive this. To set the procedure in motion, he calls on the Foreign Minister—in Washington the Secretary of State—hands over a copy of his letter of credence and asks to be received by the Head of State. In due course he is informed of the date and time of his official reception, and from then onward there are variations in procedure according to local custom.

In Washington, on the appointed day, the State Department's Chief of Protocol, accompanied by one of the President's senior military or naval aides in full-dress uniform, calls for the new ambassador in the President's car and conducts him to the White House. His family and the embassy staff follow in cars provided by the State Department. At the White House the ambassador is ushered into the President's presence, makes a short bow, and after being formally introduced by the Chief of Protocol, shakes hands with the President and presents his letter of credence. At this point it used to be customary for the new ambassador to express a few unexceptionable sentiments about his satisfaction at being in Washington and his hopes for a happy future relationship between the United States and his country, and for the President to reply in a similar vein. Nowadays both these set speeches are dispensed with—or at least they are not read out. The ambassador simply hands the President a typewritten copy of the remarks he would have made, and is in turn handed a copy of the President's reply. As a result of this short cut through protocol, President and ambassador are left free to use the time at their disposal for a short, informal chat. The ceremony ends with the ambassador's presenting his family and the embassy staff.

In London, as at most royal courts, the ceremonial is more elaborate. The new ambassador, who is called for by the Marshal of the Diplomatic Corps, is conducted to Buckingham Palace in a coach, as are his family and embassy personnel, each carriage being attended by drivers and footmen dressed in royal scarlet. At the grand entrance to the Palace the ambassador is received by the Equerry-in-Waiting, who leads him into the Grand Hall, where he is met by the Master of the Household before being conducted to the Bow Room. There he finds the Secretary of State for Foreign Affairs who, together with the Lord-in-Waiting and the Marshal of the Diplomatic Corps, eventually usher him into the presence of the Queen. After presenting him, the Marshal of the Diplomatic Corps and the Lord-in-Waiting withdraw, and he is received in private audience with only the Foreign Secretary present. Afterwards the ambassador, in his turn, presents his family and embassy personnel.

Moscow, in these matters, is as protocol-conscious as any capitalist state, republican or monarchical. It has its Chief of Protocol, who calls for the new ambassador at his embassy, and the President of the Soviet Union provides the necessary transportation, for the trip to the Kremlin. In fact, the Soviet Union has added one or two touches all its own. As the new ambassador enters the Kremlin through the Borovitsky Gate, he is met by the commandant of the Red Army Guards Contingent on duty with full military honors. Next, he is subjected to a ceremonial which requires split-second timing. Flanked by the Chief of Protocol and the principal assistant of the Soviet President, he has to enter the great Reception Hall of the Kremlin so as to meet, near the center of the vast expanse of the Hall, a procession starting simultaneously at the opposite end, led by the Soviet President and the Soviet Minister of Foreign Affairs. It is a maneuver that demands poise and a cool head for judging distances. Speeches at these ceremonies in the Kremlin are optional, but if it is agreed to have them, Soviet protocol does not, as in the White House, consider them read by a mere exchange of texts. Every word has to be spoken, and since the ambassador is expected to speak in his tongue and the Soviet President in Russian, and since both speeches are followed by a word-for-word translation into the other's language, the ceremony in these circumstances tends to be somewhat protracted.

No matter how tedious the ceremony may be, however, the formal acceptance of accreditation at last gives body and soul to an ambassador. After weeks of waiting, the envoy finally moves out of the diplomatic twilight and exists officially. He can take his rightful place among the Corps Diplomatique in the foreign capital, and it is the exact moment in which the foreign Head of State touches his letter of credence that determines his precedence among his fellow ambassadors. He may be the representative of one of the world's most powerful countries, but if the Ambassador Extraordinary and Plenipotentiary of the Grand Duchy of Luxembourg presents his credentials the day before, then Luxembourg's representative will rank above him.

161

It is an eminently sensible arrangement, which was worked out at the Congress of Vienna after the Napoleonic Wars, and it has proved itself to have many advantages, especially in our age when hardly a year passes without half a dozen countries or so rising to independence and full nationhood, all of them intensely proud of their new-found dignity and highly sensitive to the merest hint of even an imagined slight. Under the Vienna rules, power, size, riches and high-sounding titles count for nothing. Precedence is determined by rule of thumb: first come, first served—and the ambassador who has been longest in a capital automatically becomes Doyen or Dean of the Corps Diplomatique, except in some Roman Catholic countries where the Papal Nuncio traditionally speaks for the diplomatic body.

Certainly the Vienna Règlement has saved diplomats from a great deal of physical danger and the strata of society among which they move from considerable social embarrassment. Before it, precedence had depended on the relative antiquity of royal houses and monarchical titles—a far from satisfactory principle, since no king was ever prepared to concede that any royal lineage could be older than his own, and every diplomat was expected to stick up for his royal master's claims even if it meant trampling on women or children or fighting pitched battles.

In 1661, the attendants of the Spanish ambassador in London fell upon the French ambassador's coach, killed the postilion, beat up the coachman and hamstrung two horses in order to make certain that the Spanish's ambassador's coach went first. When in the following century the Swedish ambassador in London let it be known that

162

he would yield pride of place to no other envoy, not even at private gatherings, doors and corridors in quite a few houses were widened to allow him to march everywhere side by side with any other ambassador present.

But even the most elaborate precautions could not always prevent incidents of diplomatic hooliganism. All attempts by the Master of Ceremonies at the Danish Court to settle a violent dispute over seating at a royal wedding between the French and Spanish ambassadors broke down when the French ambassador announced icily, "I will give the Spanish ambassador the choice of the place which he regards as the most honorable, and when he shall have taken it, I will turn him out and take it myself."

It would be idle to pretend that the Vienna arrangement represented a long-overdue triumph of reason. The main motive behind its acceptance was fear, fear of rattling too many skeletons in Europe's royal cupboards if the arguments about ancient lineage and antiquity of title were allowed to continue after the shaking-up Napoleon had given the Old World. With Bernadotte, one of the upstart Napoleon's former Marshals, heir to the Swedish throne; with the rulers of Bavaria, Württemberg and Saxony anxious to retain the upgrading from elector to king which the plebian Corsican had graciously granted them; with the houses of Hapsburg and Bonaparte joined in marriage, disputes along the old lines were bound to prove embarrassing. It seemed much wiser to adopt a system that avoided any awkwardnesses.

Unfortunately, the Vienna Règlement has not been an unmixed blessing for diplomats, for its rules hold good for every occasion. No variation is possible. Consequently, should there be a State Opening of Parliament in the morning, a military parade in the afternoon and a banquet in the evening, the same people will always be placed next to one another in exactly the same order. If an ambassador is unlucky, he may find that, month in, month out, he is condemned to having on one side a diplomat who is stone-deaf, and on the other someone who understands and speaks no known language. Even if there is a common language, the range of topics diplomats feel they can safely discuss at these formal functions may soon be exhausted. It is hardly surprising, therefore, that ambassadors in the mass have been called the "dull-eyed diplomatic corps." Where once, in the pre-Vienna days, they faced physical danger, today they merely have to steel themselves against boredom.

Of course Vienna made no difference in diplomatic dress and manner, which continued to be dominated by court etiquette. After all, most countries in the nineteenth century were monarchies, and on ceremonial occasions diplomats almost everywhere were expected to don elaborate and braided uniforms, knee breeches, swords and magnificently plumed hats—a circumstance which caused both embarrassment and resentment among the representatives of the small number of egalitarian republics like the United States. Why, it was argued, should the men charged with conducting the business of the sovereign people of the United States of America in Europe have to submit to the pomp and flummery of royal courts?

A stout republican, Benjamin Franklin, first entered the glittering reception halls at Versailles dressed in an old coat, without a wig and leaning on a crooked, crabapple

164

cane. Louise XVI was horrified. He was prepared to support the United States if he could score a point off Britain, but he was not willing to have his court exposed to the dangerous ideas of republicanism.

Putting first things first, Benjamin Franklin decided to compromise. Aid from France, after all, was more important to him than reform in France. He designed himself a modest but elegant court costume, complete with sword, which mollified the French king without doing injury to his own convictions.

Other crowned heads in Europe were equally suspicious of the new republic's representatives, whom they regarded as little better than dangerous "agents provocateurs," and in more than one instance America's envoys were told preremptorily to stay away from court altogether unless they appeared properly attired.

Eventually, in 1817, the State Department allowed its diplomats to wear a uniform which included white knee breeches; white silk stockings; a blue, silk-lined coat; and a sword. But the concession was not popular at home where many people regarded the compromise as akin to treason. They particularly objected to the knee breeches, which they looked upon as a symbol of craven subservience to royalty.

In 1853 the opposition finally won the day. Secretary of State Mariz ordered that all United States diplomats would henceforth show their devotion to the ideals of the Republic by appearing "in the simple dress of an American citizen," which ruled out knee breeches and meant long trousers.

Europe's courts were highly displeased. In London

officials icily repeated the advice given to America's envoys earlier in the century, to stay away from Court functions. Curiously enough, Queen Victoria did not share the feeling that the future of the monarchy in Britain depended on knee breeches. She discreetly let the American envoy know that he was welcome no matter what his attire, provided he wore a sword. Otherwise, she pointed out delicately, he might be mistaken for one of her servants.

It was a shrewd observation, especially since the State Department went a step further a little later and decreed that all American representatives at foreign ceremonial functions had to wear white ties and tails and, as a final touch of sartorial republicanism, black, instead of the customary white waistcoats. From then onward, America's diplomats certainly looked strikingly different from those of other countries. Unfortunately, they also looked exactly like headwaiters in hotels and restaurants.

Mr. Joseph Hodges Choate, the American ambassador in London at the turn of the century, had the mortifying experience, on leaving a Court ball at Buckingham Palace, to be ordered by a crusty old peer resplendent in scarlet full-dress uniform, "Call me a cab."

Mr. Choate, however, was equal to the occasion. "You are a cab, sir," he replied promptly, adding with a courteous bow, "At least you are good enough not to ask me to call you a hansom cab."

In this century, of course, when most countries are republics and not monarchies, the American diplomatic practice of top hat, white tie and tails on formal occasions has become the rule rather than the exception. One of

166

the few countries that have not followed the American example is the Soviet Union.

Admittedly, Soviet diplomats immediately after the Russian Revolution in 1917 were as keen to break away from traditional diplomatic pomp and circumstance and assert their ideological differences by appearance and dress as America's representatives were after 1776. They rejected tails, morning coats and dinner jackets as bourgeois flummery. Their standard uniform for all occasions was the business suit. They even refused to call themselves ambassadors, which they rejected as a reactionary, imperialist title. Instead, they were referred to simply as "plenipotentiaries," which the irreverent soon abbreviated to "plenpots."

But the revolutionary phase in Soviet diplomacy did not last long. "Plenpots," Stalin discovered in the nineteen-thirties, come nowhere in international diplomatic protocol. They are outranked not only by ambassadors but even by the most junior minister, and since Stalin did not relish the idea of having his chief representatives abroad permanently hidden amid the mass of diplomatic small fry on all occasions, he invested them with the full style and title of "ambassador extraordinary and plenipotentiary."

The business suit, too, went by the board in due course. It may not have made Soviet diplomats look like waiters or footmen, but amid the so-called bourgeois splendors of a formal function in a foreign land, it sometimes suggested something worse—petit bourgeois clerking, which was hardly in keeping with the image of superiority that the Soviet Union sought to project after the Second World War. Consequently, Stalin set his tailors to work on designing a Soviet diplomatic uniform. What they eventually came up with was a ceremonial attire closely modeled on the full-dress uniform of a Soviet Marshal, which in weight of gold braid and expanse of epaulettes easily outclassed any capitalist creation.

Many of the new African and Asian countries which have won independence since the Second World War found a more striking and less conventional solution to the problem of diplomatic uniform than the Soviet Union —national costume; and who would deny that the general aspect presented by the assembled Corps Diplomatique in any of the world's capitals is not improved by the colorful, flowing robes of the Africans and the variety of headgear sported by the Asians! The fact that quite a few of the newly independent African countries are made up of different races and tribes and have no national costume in common has not proved an insuperable obstacle. The more expensive Paris fashion houses and the more exclusive London tailors have always shown themselves ready to run up models which, although they may not strictly speaking be national costumes, can at least be said to express the spirit of the new country. Their work in this field constitutes one of the most useful links that exist between the former imperial masters and the ex-colonial territories.

On the whole, the new African states do their best to conform to traditional diplomatic protocol, but of course the starchier rules which are so punctiliously observed in Europe have little chance of surviving in the steamy, strident capitals of awakening Africa.

Some time ago, one of the wives of Britain's representatives, entertaining one of the new African prime ministers to dinner, found herself thwarted in all her attempts to make the ladies retire to the drawing room after the meal and leave the men to their port. "We do not want to lose your charming female company," the guest of honor stated with heavy chivalry the moment she tried to leave. His hostess smiled polite acknowledgment. The guest of honor made an elaborate bow in her direction, and then, turning to his host, announced abruptly, "But if you want to talk business, go right ahead. Don't mind the women. They're too stupid to understand."

His hostess's smile did not drop by so much as a fraction of an inch. "My husband shares your view," she said brightly, "but unlike you he has never had the courage to state it quite as plainly as your Excellency."

The prime minister was delighted. "Englishwomen," he beamed, "have spirit. I like that." And ever since, Britain has had little trouble with this particular African state.

Britain's, America's and France's younger diplomats welcome the challenge presented by a posting to Africa. Their older, more conventional colleagues are understandably less keen. Not that the younger men's enthusiasm is altogether altruistic. Prospects of promotion also play their part. In the past decade Africa has sprouted more new states—and diplomatic posts—than any other continent. In 1960 alone there were no less than fourteen, and that meant that the State Department, the Foreign Office and the Quai d'Orsay had to send out fourteen new ambassadors, ministers, counselors, first secretaries and all the rest. It is a situation to delight the heart of any ambitious diplomat—and his wife. Thanks to Africa, an ambassadorship before the age of forty is no longer a mere daydream.

The African states, for their part, have to find dozens of suitable candidates to send abroad, and since they want their representatives to make a good impression, would-be diplomats and their wives are carefully initiated into the mysteries of protocol, precedence and diplomatic manners in general. They are taught how to address foreign notabilities such as the United States President ("Mr. President" or simply "Sir"), Queen Elizabeth II ("Your Majesty" once at the beginning of the conversation and after that "Ma'am," not "Madam") and foreign ambassadors ("Your Excellency"). They are told when to leave cards at other embassies and what letters to write in the lower left-hand corner of their cards on what occasion: "p.r.," which stands for "pour remercier," to thank after a dinner or a reception on the previous day; "p.f.," short for "pour féliciter," to congratulate, on a national holiday like July 4; or "p.c.," "pour condoler," to condole after a flood disaster or the death of a prominent member of the government.

At one school in Kenya, specially run for wives, pupils are introduced to the all-important rituals of cocktail and dinner parties. They learn how to mix drinks, and although their early concoctions are often fierce enough to scorch the strongest stomach lining, they usually end up by making excellent dry martinis and whisky sours. Compiling a dinner menu also frequently leads to some strange culinary combinations in the early stages of the course. One teacher had a hard time persuading an enthusiastic pupil that grilled sausages and fruit salad did not make an ideal main course despite the very attractive color appeal of the dish. But undoubtedly, the lesson the teachers find it most difficult to drive home is that it is not done in diplomatic circles to ask the wife of, say, the American, British, Italian or German ambassador how old she is, how much her husband receives by way of an expense allowance, or how many quarts of duty-free whisky or gin they both get through in a week.

It is not in Africa, however, but in West Germany that the most comprehensive guide to diplomatic behavior is to be found. Since 1956 Bonn's budding diplomats have been able to turn to *Das Buch der Etikette,* written with the help of a member of the West German Protocol Department, for advice in virtually every conceivable situation. No eventuality appears to have been omitted. With Teutonic thoroughness, the book even deals with the problem of striking up an acquaintance with an attractive lady out-of-doors without getting one's face slapped. The opening gambit consists in noting the direction in which she is walking, and then asking her for help in finding a street which one knows to be on her way. Nothing after that could be more natural than to suggest escorting her. Of course, the book insists, being a gentleman, one must then humbly confess to one's ruse and throw oneself on the lady's mercy.

There is also voluminous advice on such diverse subjects as lighting (indirect is preferred to direct lighting because it is kinder to women), the use of lavatories in small apartments which may not be soundproof, the carrying of umbrellas and the excessive application of highly scented after-shave lotions. All the sweet-smelling toiletries from Paris, the book decrees, are no substitute for a daily bath or shower. And as if to anticipate opposition to ablutions on a regular daily basis, the book asks rhetorically, "Do you not know the exciting, thrilling sense of well-being that results from a complete wash and scrub?"

Plainly, aspiring diplomats do not suffer from a shortage of advice on how to behave. And if they should feel that there is too much and that they would like just one basic rule to guide them, they can do no better than to recall the brief and succinct instruction Napoleon gave to one of his ambassadors: "Keep a good table and look after the ladies."

13:

A "DPL"-Plated
Existence

ONE OF THE FIRST ACTS OF ANY DIPLOMAT, ON ARRIVING in a foreign capital to begin his job of representing his country, is to put special plates on his car—"DPL" in Washington and "C.D." (Corps Diplomatique) everywhere else. They are a symbol of his special status. They mean that if he chooses to ignore traffic lights, exceed the speed limits, drive on the wrong side of the road or park in a no-parking area, there is nothing the local police can do about it. He cannot be arrested. Even the highest court in the land cannot touch him.

It all began long before the dawn of the motor car age in the days when kings were absolute and could do no wrong, and their representatives were considered extensions of their royal masters' sacrosanct personages and

173

therefore inviolate. And it has survived because diplomats must, it is claimed, be free to concentrate on looking after their nation's interests without fear of interference or pressure on them by anyone in the country where they are stationed.

Since pressure nowadays can take many subtle forms, the list of immunities and privileges enjoyed by diplomats en poste abroad is inevitably extensive. They cannot be sued, prosecuted or taxed. The customs officer cannot go through their luggage, nor the tax inspector through their earnings. Landlords have no means of enforcing payment of rent by them, nor stores of bills. They are exempt from purchase or sales tax, customs charges, excise duties and license fees for cars, guns, hunting or fishing. They can smoke and drink themselves silly for a comparatively small outlay. Without duty, many of the choicest wines and liqueurs cost only a fraction of the usual across-the-counter shop price. The apartments or houses where they and their families live are truly their castles, for like the embassies or legations where they work, their private residences are extraterritorial, and no one can enter without their consent. When the Soviet embassy in Ottawa caught fire in 1956, the local fire chief, who had rushed to the scene with over a hundred of his men, had to stand by helplessly while the Russians removed their archives. By the time consent was eventually given, the building was beyond saving.

Moreover, should tensions and frustrations build up despite this care- and pressure-free existence, diplomats can safely let off steam, kicking policemen or blowing up public monuments. The law is powerless. All diplomats have to do if their carryings-on are challenged is to prove that they are on the list of foreign diplomats which the Foreign Ministry of every host country keeps. In Washington the State Department nowadays thoughtfully provides foreign diplomats with identification cards, certifying their status, to avoid a repetition of incidents like the one in which a highway patrolman many years ago brusquely brushed aside the claim to immunity by the Iranian Minister with the curt comment that he had heard of Baptist ministers but never of Iranian ministers.

Diplomatic immunity continues even after death. If a diplomat commits suicide, no coroner or magistrate is entitled to examine his corpse or any notes he may have left.

Presented with this solid wall of protection and privilege, many people will wonder whether they should ever allow themselves to become involved with diplomats in any way. Why rent houses to them, sell them goods or have them round for dinner when they can cheat, swindle and brawl with immunity?

Fortunately there is no need to take quite so gloomy a view. Governments, after all, send out diplomats to foster good will abroad, and they are naturally anxious not to have their purpose defeated by representatives who choose to misbehave. If a Third Secretary attached to a foreign embassy in Washington, for instance, is caught roaring down Main Street somewhere at ninety miles per hour in a low-slung sports car, the State Department is likely to hear about it sooner or later—if only because the local police department will want to check his claim to immunity. "State," while confirming his claim, will go through its files to see if there are reports of other, similar offenses against the young man, and if so, will discreetly pass the word along to his embassy. Before very long, a peremptory summons from the ambassador will herald a carpeting compared with which an appearance in a traffic court would seem almost painless. At best he will be told to sell his sports car and get himself something more respectable and slower, and at worst that if there is one more offense, he will have "outlived his usefulness in his present post."

Embassies are equally sensitive at the slightest suggestion of possible debt bilking. A diplomat's wife who refuses to pay for a gown which has not been altered to her satisfaction may discover that her husband has to explain her shopping habits and her wardrobe to his superiors. Diplomatic immunity, in fact, often deprives those who enjoy it of the privilege of settling their private affairs on their own and without the boss's knowing.

Nor is it easy for a diplomat to use his duty-free alcohol and tobacco privilege to set up an undercover business in competition with the local trade. He cannot simply buy the stuff at any store, bar or restaurant. If he does, he must pay the ordinary price, with full tax and duty, like everyone else—as an Asian diplomat found out to his cost when he desperately tried to reduce his not inconsiderable check in a New York night club by trying to knock duty and tax off the two dozen bottles of champagne he and his party had consumed.

To be duty-free, his wine and tobacco must come from a bonded warehouse. There must be a formal order, which for the benefit of the local customs and excise officials must certify the diplomatic status of the applicant. Although this procedure is a mere formality, it affords

176

the officials of the host country a discreet opportunity to keep an eye on the drinking and smoking habits of members of the Corps Diplomatique.

Fortunately, the officials who perform this delicate task are in most countries unusually understanding and broadminded. Two or three bottles-a-day men among diplomats do not surprise them in the least, but if a young attaché at the Ruritanian embassy orders enough champagne once a week to float a battleship, they will gently draw the attention of the Ruritanian embassy to the excessively heavy burden of entertainment that appears to be borne by a junior member of their staff.

In days gone by, some of the more robust ambassadors had no qualms about punishing their staff on the spot. In 1603, when the Duc de Sully, who had come to London from France on a special embassy, learned that a member of his entourage had been involved in a fight in which an Englishman had been killed, he promptly had the man arrested and tried, with himself as judge, jury and prosecutor. Concluding that the man was guilty, he decided, in the interests of enforcing good behavior among his staff, to make an example of him, and condemned him to be beheaded.

The outside world might have heard nothing of these proceedings if the noble Duke had not discovered at the last moment that he lacked the one person who could give effect to his decision—an executioner. Determined to press on, however, he sent a courteous note to the Lord Mayor of London, presenting his compliments and humbly begging His Worship to be kind enough to lend him the City of London's executioner for a little while.

177

The Lord Mayor was appalled. Even as lofty a personage as the French ambassador should not, he felt, set up his own court of law on English soil, and after a great deal of polite argument the Duke was eventually persuaded to hand his prisoner into the custody of James I, who graciously pardoned him.

Nowadays, junior diplomats are less at the mercy of juridically-minded ambassadors. They can be reported on, reprimanded, severely reprimanded or packed off home, but they cannot have their heads cut off or be locked up as prisoners in their embassy. Nor, for that matter, can anyone else who steps onto the "extraterritorial" soil of an embassy. Still, if the embassy represents an authoritarian regime, and he happens to belong to its known enemies, he would be wise to let his friends know of any proposed visits beforehand and not to put his trust altogether in international law and practice. For though the law is clear, its enforcement is less so, since embassies and legations enjoy complete immunity and cannot be entered without permission, no matter what the circumstances.

Sun Yat-Sen, the founder of the Kuomintang, who had fled to London to escape the attentions of the Imperial Chinese authorities, failed to take that elementary precaution when he visited the Chinese legation in 1896. He was promptly seized and locked up in an attic to await the arrival of a Chinese boat in the Port of London to take him back to China. From his window he could see the houses and gardens next door, but he knew it was useless shouting for help. His captors would knock him out before he had a chance to attract anyone's attention, let alone explain his plight. Fortunately, he managed to find a scrap of paper, scribble a message for a friend on it and, having wrapped it around a paperweight, throw it far enough so that it landed in a garden just beyond the legation wall.

As luck would have it, no one in the legation had seen the operation, but someone outside had. The message was picked up and delivered without delay. But even then, Sun Yat-Sen's troubles were not over. When his friend applied for a writ of habeus corpus, the High Court told him with regret that, though the Imperial Chinese minister was acting illegally, he was not subject to its jurisdiction.

The British Government thereupon took a hand in the matter and gave the minister twenty-four hours to release his prisoner. That did the trick. Sun Yat-Sen was freed to topple the Manchus off their throne in 1911 and become the first head of the new Chinese Republic.

What the British Government could have done if the minister had not caved in is not quite clear. It could, of course, have broken off diplomatic relations, or it could have laid siege to the legation. Today that would undoubtedly be a highly effective weapon, since embassies are no longer virtually self-contained communities and have to rely on their water, electricity and power supplies from outside. But the British authorities could certainly not have broken into the legation. The extraterritoriality of diplomatic missions is sacrosanct. There is no way round it, except a waiver by the ambassador or his government.

When a group of anti-Communist Rumanians burst into the legation of the Rumanian People's Democracy in Bern in 1955, seized the building and unceremoniously kicked the Communist staff out into the street, the Swiss police

179

and military could not begin operations to eject the intruders and reinstall the rightful owners until they had been given permission to set foot on the diplomatically immune soil of the legation.

The formalities surrounding immunity and waivers can sometimes produce strange results. In 1929 a Soviet counselor who was afraid of being liquidated fled from his embassy in Paris and sought French police protection. Unfortunately, the Russian Secret Service men in the embassy got wind of his defection, seized his wife and child, and took them to the embassy. The distracted counselor appealed for help to the French Foreign Office, but no one there could think of anything more helpful than a formal protest to the Soviet government—until a bright young official from the Protocol Department arrived on the scene.

"Your ambassador is away on leave at the moment?" he asked the Russian. The counselor nodded agreement.

"And you have not been formally dismissed or recalled by your government?", the Frenchman continued.

The Russian shook his head. "That is not the way," he explained glumly, "in which the Soviets work in cases like this when they want to liquidate you. They want no fuss, no publicity."

"Quite so." The Frenchman nodded briskly. "Then you are still officially counselor at the Soviet embassy and as such—according to my diplomatic list—the Number Two there. Consequently, in your ambassador's absence, you are in charge. Would you, therefore, mind signing this paper to authorize our police to enter your embassy and use such force as may be necessary to release your wife and child!"

The counselor and his family were reunited within the hour.

So complete is the protection afforded by diplomatic premises that it is not surprising that many people who are not diplomats try to take advantage of it.

In Latin America, for instance, it is standard practice for the leaders of the losing side in any revolution to seek asylum in a foreign embassy. The whole business is very simple. The moment the president, or the revolutionary leader, as the case may be, realizes that his side is not going to make it, he heads for the nearest embassy— usually one belonging to a Latin American sister republic —and stays holed up there until the last shot has been fired in the fighting outside. It is an accepted convention in Latin American revolutions that embassies are never touched, no matter how fierce the battle may be. Once the issue is definitely decided, the ambassador who is providing asylum for the leaders of the losing side calls on the victors and asks for safe-conducts for his protégés out of the country. The request is never refused, because no Latin American leader deludes himself, even in his moment of triumph, into believing that his revolution is likely to be the last. The ambassador returns to his embassy. Shortly afterwards, he discreetly conducts his "guests" in person to the nearest airport and a waiting aircraft which whisks them out of the country. Neither along their route nor at the airport is there any sign of the mobs that are howling for their blood almost everywhere else. It is, in fact, as smooth a way of retiring a man from active politics as elevation to the House of Lords in Britain.

The United States does not share the enthusiasm of its American sister republics for this procedure and resents having its embassies and legations turned into places of refuge. In former days this attitude primarily stemmed from a reluctance to become drawn into other nations' affairs, but it persists even today when the United States is deeply involved in many parts of the world. The State Department does not want to see a privilege, intended to help diplomats discharge their duties properly, treated as a convenience by politicians down on their luck.

Exceptions are made, of course, but only in rare cases where a man is in imminent danger of his life. Cardinal Mindszenty was granted asylum in the United States legation in Budapest in 1956 when Russian tanks, contrary to undertakings indicated, rolled back into town to crush the Hungarian uprising and the Imre Nagy government. Since it has not so far proved possible to work out any arrangements which would satisfactorily guarantee the Cardinal's safety if he were to set foot outside the United States legation, he has remained there ever since. Imre Nagy and his colleagues, who had sought refuge in the Yugoslav legation and had later been induced to leave its protection under a safe conduct to travel to Yugoslavia, were seized before they had driven farther than a few hundred yards, bundled away to prison, and a few months afterwards executed.

Perhaps the most unusual, and certainly the most massive, request for asylum ever made in diplomatic history

182

came many years ago from a eunuch of the Imperial Court of the Shah in Teheran.

One morning he presented himself to the British minister there and announced that all was not well between the illustrious occupant of the Peacock Throne and his wives. The Shah apparently had fallen in love again and proposed to take unto himself yet another wife. Not—the eunuch hastened to explain—that his wives objected to periodic additions to their number; they knew their station in life too well for that. What they did object to in this case was the addition of a girl who was the sister of one of the wives he had already. That was too much. It was against custom and tradition, and they had to seek sanctuary against their imperial master's whims in a foreign legation. Would the British minister please oblige?

The British minister in this instance appears to have been a diplomat of exceptionally deep understanding and human warmth. He declared himself honored at this proof of the ladies' confidence in him and put himself and his legation at their disposal. It was only toward the end of the interview that his smooth urbanity received a slight jolt when he inquired politely how many ladies he would have the privilege of playing host to. After making a brief calculation, the eunuch announced that there would be about three hundred.

Still, having given his word, the minister felt that he could not back down. He ordered tents to be pitched on the vast legation lawn, and his servants were dispatched to buy up all the sheep and bread they could lay their hands on. Within two hours the legation was ready to receive the ladies.

But, alas, they never arrived. At the last minute, as they were about to leave his palace, the Shah had given in—no doubt a bitter pill for him, but better by far than having the King of Kings, the successor of the mighty Xerxes and Darius, publicly exposed before all his subjects as a man who could not stop even his own womenfolk from walking out on him.

Since that narrow escape from having one of His Majesty's legations transformed into a harem, Britain has tended to be as cautious as the United States in using the extraterritorial status of its overseas establishments. The general ruling is that the immunities, rights and privileges conferred on diplomats by international law and custom are for their benefit and no one else's.

Of course diplomats serving their countries abroad derive benefits not only from international law and custom but also from their home governments, which frequently treat them with a generosity other government employees envy. They are given travel allowances, rent allowances (to permit them to take apartments in the more exclusive districts, when they are not provided with official accommodation), dress allowances, and entertainment allowances. The British Foreign Office helps with school fees, a practice now followed by the State Department. The wives of senior French diplomats are dressed by Dior or other famous Paris fashion houses at little or no cost, and their kitchens are run by some of France's most inspired chefs —which explains why no one in Washington, London, Rome or Moscow has ever been known to turn down a dinner invitation from the French ambassador. And they are supplied often with food and drink from home, at reduced prices, especially in the more outlandish places. In this last respect the United States has gone further than any other country. Special stores for its diplomats exist not only in places like Kabul or Seoul but in cities like London, Paris and Bonn, where it is perfectly easy to buy all the meat, fish and vegetables that are needed. The result is that many United States diplomats, especially in the lower ranks, tend to live, work and eat as they would in America, with little real contact with the local population.

It is a practice which President Kennedy has condemned. "Instead of becoming merely experts in diplomatic history or in current clippings of the *New York Times,*" he told Foreign Service officers in May, 1962, "you have to involve yourselves in every element of foreign life— labor, the class struggle, cultural affairs, and all the rest— attempting to predict in what direction the forces will move."

These are unexceptionable precepts, but of course the special stores are cheaper than the local shops. Moreover, what are you to do with your professors, writers, youth leaders and trade union officials once you have made contact with them? Even they like to eat and drink occasionally. In fact, as every diplomat knows, they talk better when they are well entertained. And on entertainment, unfortunately, Congress tends to come down on the mean side. The total allowances it votes United States representatives abroad are smaller than those of either Britain or West Germany. At some United States embassy receptions the mountains of Soviet caviar and oceans of Caucasian champagne can be matched only by a limited number of trays of canapes and a trickle of indifferent wine. United States diplomats without private means have to shun entertaining in the grand style and stretch their entertainment budget by judicious entertaining privately in their homes.

But though America's representatives have their worries in keeping up with the diplomatic Joneses, none of them would deny that they are better off than United States government servants at home. And when the time comes to return and do a tour of duty in the United States, most of them view the prospect with distaste. For, as in the case of every diplomat stationed abroad to represent his country, a posting home brings his Cinderella-like existence to an end.

The customs officer at the last foreign frontier will wave him and his family on, saluting smartly, without so much as a glance at his pile of suitcases, but to the customs officer of his own country he and his wife are just another "Mr. and Mrs. John Citizen." As he goes through their baggage, he will carefully note every item on which duty is payable.

Gone at one fell blow are all the immunities and privileges that made life so pleasant abroad; and so are the rent, dress, travel and entertainment allowances, as well as freedom from the attentions of the tax inspector.

Small wonder, therefore, that returning diplomats are often in a state of shock in the first few days and find it difficult to summon a smile as they say, "It's good to be back home!"

14:

The United Nations

THE WEST AND EAST FRONTS OF THE TALL UNITED NATIONS headquarters building on New York's East River, a few blocks from Times Square and Broadway, are covered with glass. There are 5,400 windows, and it takes five men two weeks to clean them all. "And when we've finished, we start again. It's a continuous operation," they explain, completely impervious to all the stone-throwing that goes on inside.

To a visitor making his first tour of the United Nations, these five men seem to be the only ones with a clear purpose. Everyone else, delegates and members of the Secretariat, appear to be entirely absorbed in a strange world of their own. Which of course the United Nations is. Technically, it is not part of New York City, and no New York policeman can make an arrest there.

It is a confusing place. In the immense Assembly Hall, with its starkly simple backdrop of the leaf-rimmed United Nations emblem high above the Presidential dais, the visitor may be astonished to find the majority of this planet's delegates dozing away peacefully as the burning issues of the day are laid before them in speech after speech—until he discovers that they have all had advance copies but have to listen in person all the same because diplomatic courtesy demands it.

In the Security Council he may witness a sharp, bitter altercation between Mr. Adlai Stevenson and Mr. Zorin. And in the thickly carpeted lounges and lobbies the air may seem heavy with plotting and scheming as delegates huddle together in tiny, animated groups, exchanging whispered confidences. By the time he leaves, he may wonder whether he has seen a world parliament in embryo or a madhouse.

The United Nations, of course, is neither. Basically, it is no more than an international conference of one hundred and ten independent sovereign nations in permanent session. Yet the lofty ideals expressed in the preamble of its Charter lift it above ordinary international conferences. They compel it to aim high, yet it can do only as much, or as little, as its member governments want it to. And its "little" can be minuscule. The United Nations is always in danger of producing nothing but resolutions.

The idea was that the Security Council, consisting of five permanent members—the United States, the Soviet

188

Union, Great Britain, France and Nationalist China—and six nonpermanent members serving a two-year term—should take action whenever peace was threatened anywhere. Since the five permanent members were each given the right to veto anything they disapproved of, and since nearly every proposal has been disapproved of by one of them, the Security Council has rarely been in a position to order "All Systems Go!" When it did, as in the case of Communist aggression in Korea, the principal veto-wielder, the Soviet Union, happened to be absent.

The General Assembly was not built for action, either. Admittedly, none of its members, not even the biggest and most powerful, has a right to veto its decisions, but decisions are not easily arrived at in a body that has risen steadily in size from fifty to sixty, eighty and eventually over a hundred members. Even the simplest resolution on the most innocuous topic bears the unmistakable stamp of compromise between scores of conflicting viewpoints. Indeed, so strenuous is the process that, once a text is agreed and every saving clause and qualification carefully incorporated, many delegates can hardly summon the energy to vote on it, let alone initiate further action.

The only person who cannot sit back and accept votes and resolutions as the end product of United Nations activity is the Secretary General. In 1945 no one had any very clear idea about what his job was actually going to be. The Great Powers hoped that he would turn out to be a nice, quiet, international civil servant, rather like the Secretaries-General of the old League of Nations, with few ideas of his own, who would confine himself to carrying out the instructions of the Security Council and the

General Assembly and not be seen or heard of for the rest of the time. Certainly they firmly set their face against personality candidates like Eisenhower, Smuts, Eden, Schweitzer, Lester Pearson or Nehru, whose names were occasionally canvassed. What they wanted were safe, relatively unknown men from small, comparatively uncommitted countries. They first picked Trygvie Lie from Norway, which did not break with its traditional policy of neutrality in peacetime by joining NATO until some years after his election: then Dag Hammarskjold, a little-known civil servant from neutral Sweden; and thirdly, U Thant, a career diplomat from neutralist Burma.

All of them seemed sound, reliable men when they were first elected, not likely to disturb diplomacy's set ways with newfangled notions about world government. But the job had its own dynamism. It made and molded its occupants, thrusting them willy-nilly to the center of the international stage.

After Trygvie Lie and his spectacular but unsuccessful attempts to resolve Cold War differences between East and West, Dag Hammarskjold at first appeared shy and retiring, an almost colorless personality, with little or no influence on events. The leaders of the Great Powers showed no inclination to consult him, and he seemed content to stay in the background, reluctant to proffer advice unless asked.

It was a phase that did not last long. First the Suez crisis, later the 1958 troubles in the Lebanon and Jordan, and finally the Congo crisis dramatically altered his position. His office on the thirty-eighth floor of the United Nations Headquarters in New York suddenly became the meeting place for the high and mighty of this world. If there were differences, it was left to him to find a formula to bridge them. If action was demanded, he was asked to draft a plan. Having seen and talked to everyone, only he could make sense of the vaguely worded, oracular resolutions, often months old, issuing forth from the Security Council and the General Assembly from time to time. Only he knew the wishes and reservations of every government. He alone could strike a balance between what could and what could not be attempted. Like his predecessor, Trygvie Lie, and his successor, U Thant, he became the key man in every United Nations operation. He could not help being drawn in. His office left him no choice.

Yet the limits of the Secretary General's powers are curiously vague. He will claim that the authority for his initiatives and actions flows from "the principles of the United Nations," but he will quickly come a cropper if his interpretation of those principles is not backed by a powerful combination of member countries. Hammarskjold had that backing during the Middle East crises and in the Congo; he did not have it, and consequently failed, when in 1961 he offered to mediate between President Bourguiba and General de Gaulle after fighting had broken out between French and Tunisian troops around the French naval base at Bizerte.

President Bourguiba had provoked the crisis, and General de Gaulle, who contemptuously dismisses the whole United Nations as "ce machin," that "thingumajig," had no intention of allowing Hammarskjold to get him off the hook. Furthermore, neither the United States nor Britain was prepared to bring pressure on de Gaulle at a time when he had on his hands the far more important and delicate task of ending the Algerian crisis.

Nevertheless, Hammarskjold pressed on. He drove to Bizerte, only to have his car searched by French paratroopers. When he protested that he was entitled to diplomatic immunity, a French officer turned to a paratroop sergeant and asked, "Who is Hammarskjold, anyway?" The admiral commanding the French naval base refused to receive him, and when he offered to fly to Paris for talks with de Gaulle, he was told, "The Secretary General has been informed of the point of view of the French government by a note which will render his voyage to Paris unnecessary."

A Secretary General forgets the true sources of his authority at his peril. His job is a constant struggle to make high-minded idealism and practical politics work in harness.

The problem presents itself in all sorts of guises—not least in the hiring of staff for the Secretariat. Ideally, of course, the Secretary General should be able to get the best man for every one of the 4,400 jobs in the Secretariat, irrespective of nationality. In practice, he would not last a week if he and his personnel department handed out jobs on ability alone. Every member country wants to see some of its nationals on the Secretariat, and there are always complaints from this or that country that it is "under-represented."

Naturally, the Secretary General points out in reply that the members of the Secretariat do not "represent" the country they came from, but that they are international civil servants, who must not take instructions from

192

their governments' delegations and who owe their allegiance to the light-blue United Nations flag, with its polar projection of the world in white—which, as anyone arriving at United Nations Headquarters is bound to notice, is symbolically placed a little higher than the national flags of member countries.

Having made his point of principle, however, he is then bound to trim his sails to the winds of political reality, and hope that the new people who are taken on will soon become imbued with the esprit de corps which the Secretariat has developed over the years. Not that it is easy to take on new people to achieve a national and geographical balance. The Communist bloc countries complain, whenever it suits them, that they are unfairly and overwhelmingly outnumbered by nationals from America and America's military blocs, but the jobs already allocated to them—just under a hundred in the top echelon of the Secretariat alone—are often left vacant by them for months on end. The reason for these gaps is that their people are frequently recalled abruptly after only about two years' service, and sometimes less, as though they were in imminent danger of contamination through overexposure to the United Nations atmosphere.

Recruitment among the Afro-Asians, too, bristles with difficulties. If the Secretary General or his principal aides discover in Africa or Asia a man they would like to have in the Secretariat, he will probably turn out to be one of the tiny handful of trained diplomats, civil servants, administrators or scientists most new countries need to begin life, and his government will be loath to see him go, even for a short period. If, on the other hand, the Secretariat

193

finds itself under pressure to accept a certain candidate, there may prove to be some substance to the shadow of suspicion that his motives are less than pure. After all, while United Nations salaries, allowances and "fringe benefits," starting at the top with the Secretary General's seventy thousand dollars a year tax-free, may be barely adequate by American standards and no more than generous by European standards, they are positively lavish by African and Asian standards.

Still, the Personnel Department of the United Nations generally manages to cope with any little awkwardnesses, though of course not always entirely to its own satisfaction.

On one occasion an African chief of state was very keen to secure a job for one of his nephews. The Personnel did their best to stall. Many new countries had been admitted to the United Nations recently, they explained, and there were so few jobs in the Secretariat. Perhaps the nephew would be good enough to fill out an application form, and he would be put on a waiting list. All went well until someone added that in any case the only jobs that were expected to fall vacant in the near future were highly specialized and would require extensive qualifications. At that the chief exploded.

"Qualifications!" he roared. "For years my people have been denied political rights on the excuse that they lacked the qualifications to run their own affairs. And now the United Nations uses the same excuse. Perhaps Mr. Krushchev is right about the imperialist control of this Organization." The Personnel people knew they were beaten.

Once a man joins the Secretariat, he is not likely to find himself working next to people from his own country, for the aim is to mix up nationalities as thoroughly as possible. If a department head is Canadian or Brazilian, his deputy will be Indian or Belgian, and the next in seniority Australian or Moroccan.

The trouble with this system is that it calls for a high degree of harmonization in office routine; and although the preponderance of American typists and secretaries helps to produce some measure of uniformity, this is not proving easy. Scandinavian administrators tend to put every little thing down on paper. The Italians, by contrast, are much more casual, never commit themselves on paper if they can help it and seldom bother to file other people's memoranda. The Dutch always "go through the proper channels," punctiliously consulting their superiors at every stage. With the French it is almost a point of honor to bypass superiors.

United Nations officials learned to take these inconveniences in their stride. They know life only becomes really difficult for them when, by the corporate will of their political masters, the Security Council and the General Assembly, they are pitched into something like the Congo operation. Suddenly a man nurtured in the comparative calm of career diplomacy or the civil service, and with little administrative, military or political experience, may find himself administering a province the size of France and Germany combined, commanding military forces, and trying to do deals with some of the world's most erratic politicians.

He may be despatched to Elizabethville, the capital of the break-away province of Katanga, with instructions to secure an agreement between President Tshombe and the

Central Congolese government in Leopoldville. If so, he is only one of many, but the broad pattern of these missions seldom varies.

Shortly after arrival in Elizabethville, he calls on the Katangese President and discovers to his surprise that far from being an ogre, Tschombe is a man of considerable charm. He gingerly produces his draft for an agreement, and just as he braces himself for a lengthy point by point argument, the President, after the briefest glance at the document, declares himself in full accord with every sentence in it. A meeting with the Leopoldville government, he adds, ought to be arranged within the next week or so.

Two or three hours later, the interview ends and the United Nations official leaves, aglow with whisky and the prospects of early success. All seems well until next morning. Just as he is about to board his aircraft at Elizabethville airport for Leopoldville to arrange the final peace meeting, he sees President Tshombe arrive. The President greets him like a long-lost friend, and explains that he is just off to Geneva for a cure for a month or two.

The United Nations official protests. What about the meeting he was asked to arrange? he demands.

President Tshombe waves to him gaily as he moves away briskly, and the United Nations official just catches his parting words, telling him not to worry; his Minister of the Interior, who enjoys his fullest confidence, will deal with everything.

In Leopoldville the United Nations official discovers, of course, that nobody in the Central Congolese government has the slightest confidence in Tshombe's Minister of the

Interior. The man is a criminal, he is told, and there is a warrant out for his arrest.

Gradually the United Nations official discovers that everyone in the Congo has a warrant out for everyone else, and when he suggests—not unreasonably—that as a first step toward reconciliation all these warrants ought to be withdrawn, he is informed that his proposal amounts to an intolerable interference in the internal affairs of the Congo.

By this stage the United Nations official is well and truly launched on the road of frustration which will sooner or later lead him to the brink of nervous exhaustion.

The Congo has used up United Nations officials at an alarming rate, and since the end of 1961 the Organization has found it increasingly difficult to find replacements, the more so since anyone sent to the French-speaking Congo must know French well enough to be able to hold his own in any argument in which he may become involved with the soldiery of the Central government's Force Publique or President Tshombe's Gendarmerie. Inability to cope with such contingencies can mean a beating up or worse.

Even with French, however, the safety of United Nations officials hangs by a slender thread. Some time ago a Tunisian member of the United Nations was accosted by two Congolese soldiers and accused of being a white imperialist, a suppressor of colonial people.

The Tunisian protested. "I'm not an imperialist. I'm a Tunisian."

The Congolese soldiers looked unconvinced. "What's a Tunisian?"

197

"My country, like yours, lies in Africa. It was ruled by the French for many years, just as yours was ruled by the Belgians. But for over three years now we have been independent."

The two Congolese soldiers took their time digesting the explanation. Eventually one of them shook his head in wonderment and said, "Independent for only three years, and you're white already."

For the soldiers sent to the Congo on behalf of the United Nations, conditions are often more confusing and frustrating than for the civilians. From the purely military point of view the most sensible way of keeping order would have been to send a large national contingent trained to work and to fight as one unit, but if the Americans had been chosen for the task, the Russians would have insisted on also despatching troops, and the purpose of United Nations intervention—to isolate the Congo's troubles from the Cold War—would have been defeated. Consequently only troops from uncommitted nations could be sent, at an inevitably high price in military efficiency.

Their total strength throughout the Congo operation has hovered between sixteen thousand and seventeen thousand, but their composition is a military commander's nightmare—from contingents of a few thousand in the case of India and Ethiopia to units of a few hundred in the case of Ghana, Sweden and Sierra Leone. They speak different languages, use different equipment and have been trained on widely different drill manuals. If they go into action together, they are liable to be of more danger to one another than to their opponents. If one unit runs out of ammunition, it cannot borrow from its neighbors. And the system of communications, by which instructions and information are passed between units and up the chain of command and back again, is at best erratic—especially when, as in many cases, authority has to come all the way from New York.

Inevitably, commanding officers in the field have to devise their own ways of dealing with local crises. In one instance an Indian battalion charged with holding the perimeter of an airfield for the United Nations found itself regularly bombarded by mortar fire night after night after a spotter aircraft, piloted by an anti-U.N. "mercenary," had flown low over its positions the previous afternoon. Its commanding officer asked higher authority for permission to return the mortar fire but was refused. United Nations troops, he was told, were not to fire "indiscriminately." He next requested permission to shoot down the spotter aircraft, but was again refused, this time on the ground that since the plane had, according to his report, no markings, its hostility was merely a matter of supposition.

It so happened that the Indian officer knew the bar the pilot frequented on most evenings, and he consequently decided to take the law into his own hands. He sought the pilot out and told him that he had ordered his men to shoot him down if he ever flew across their positions again.

The pilot laughed. "But you have been refused permission, colonel. I can defy the United Nations, but you, in your position, will be court-martialed."

"I know." The Indian smiled pleasantly. "But you won't have the satisfaction of reading about it."

The spotter aircraft was not seen again.

For many United Nations soldiers, the most unsettling aspect of their service in the Congo is to find that their efforts win them not praise but abuse. At one time or another most units have had charges of misbehavior, brutality and theft—and even of committing atrocities—flung at them. The Ghurkas have been called "pagan pygmies from the foothills of the Himalayas," although they, at least, had the satisfaction of rescuing the man who coined that phrase from the tender mercies of some of President Tshombe's drunken gendarmes. But there has been dismay and consternation whenever any country has threatened to withdraw its contingent. All of a sudden the soldiers' services are appreciated, often admittedly for no better reason than that no one can think of any alternative way.

This may not be the most positive encouragement for United Nations servants, but they are likely to get no other. And on the basis of past experience, they can console themselves by paraphrasing the Roman emperor Tiberius's famous remark, "We care not what they say of us, so long as they take note of us."

Abuse as well as use are all grist to the United Nations mill. The one thing the Organization cannot survive is indifference. In this sense, even Mr. Krushchev turned out to be a good United Nations man when he descended on its Headquarters by the East River in New York late in 1960.

Of course, that was not his intention. But having torpedoed the Paris Summit Conference after the U2 affair and announced that he would have no further dealings with the Eisenhower administration, he discovered that

200

he had declared a virtual moratorium on all international activity until the new American administration was installed in January, 1961. In fact, for more than half a year, he had by his own actions left himself with nothing to do in foreign affairs, with no room for manoeuver backwards, forwards or sideways—an uncomfortable position for someone who was under constant fire from his own Stalinists and from Peking. He had somehow to give an impression of energy and vitality, even if he did not move. And the platform he chose for his act was the United Nations General Assembly.

As a result, every head of government who could lay his hands on a ship or an aircraft headed for New York. All of them had previously decided to give that year's Assembly a miss, but they could not afford to let Krushchev bag the stage. The United Nations had never seen such a galaxy. Foreign ministers counted for nothing. Ambassadors, extraordinary and plenipotentiary, were merely indistinct faces in the crowd. Tito, Nasser, Soekarno, Macmillan, Nehru, Eisenhower, Diefenbaker, Nkrumah, Castro, Makarios—they were all there.

It did not matter that nothing positive was achieved. It did not even matter that Krushchev banged his desk with his shoe and called the United Nations "a branch of the State Department;" Eisenhower "a liar;" the Philippine delegate "a jerk and a lackey;" and Dag Hammarskjold, whose resignation he demanded, "a fool." It did not matter that he interrupted Macmillan or insisted on the replacement of the Secretary General by a troika. It was irrelevant that he later apologized to the Philippine delegate, describing him as an old parliamentarian and himself as a young one; expressed his appreciation for the lessons in parliamentarianism he had had from Nepal— wondering at the same time whether there was a parliament in Nepal—or on his return to Moscow branded the whole of the United Nations as "a terrible organization" where "they get much money and spend much time in restaurants with their wives."

What did matter to the United Nations was that the Soviet leader's antics made it front page news throughout the world for more than four weeks. He may only have treated it as convenience for his own purposes, but convenience is habit-forming. Two years later, in 1962, at the height of the Cuban crisis, he raised no objections when U Thant, the Acting Secretary General, on his own initiative opened up the way for direct negotiations between President Kennedy and himself. And a few weeks later he quickly forgot his passionate advocacy of the troika arrangement and ordered his man at the United Nations to support U Thant's election to substantive rank. After all, a single and independent Secretary General had just proved his usefulness in what might otherwise have been a very nasty situation.

In the view of many African and Asian countries, the existence of the United Nations bestows a less fleeting benefit. It makes diplomacy cheaper. Why incur the enormous expense of running embassies and legations all over the world in nearly sixscore nations if you can find their representatives conveniently gathered in one spot? Mali, Guinea, the Ivory Coast and Tanganyika have already announced that they intend to concentrate their diplomatic representation abroad at the United Nations and virtually ignore the world's capitals. Others will no doubt follow suit, and in due course the Great Powers may have to turn their United Nations delegations into miniature foreign ministries to cope with the trend.

The people in the United Nations building whose reactions to these developments is one of undiluted delight are the salesmen in the souvenir shop on the ground floor. Business obviously will continue to be good. As it is, they do a roaring trade in carvings, dolls in national costumes, paintings and folk-lore trinkets. Only recently, Arab camel saddles became one of their best-selling lines. Apparently many New Yorkers felt that they encouraged the ideal sitting posture for watching television.

15:

Agencies and Initials

NO COUNTRY, THESE DAYS, CAN LIVE IN ISOLATION. ANYONE who doubts how interdependent we are has only to add up the number of international bodies in the world today —almost three score and ten at the latest count.

Of course, not all these organizations were set up within the last generation. The origins of the Universal Postal Union go back to the last century, and the Central Commission for the Navigation of the Rhine can trace its ancestry to the Congress of Vienna after the end of the Napoleonic Wars. But it was not until after the Second World War that international organizations really started sprouting all over the place. Indeed, so great is their number that what a student of world affairs nowadays needs above everything else is a good head for initials.

UNO is simple. So is NATO, and with practice one soon gets used to SEATO, the South East Asia Treaty Organization. But CENTO is already more difficult. Originally known as the Baghdad Pact Organization, its aim is to halt Soviet expansion in the Near and Middle East. Unfortunately, the revolutionary regime of General Kassim, which seized power in Iraq in 1958, would have nothing to do with it. Its headquarters had to be rapidly moved out of Baghdad to Ankara and it was renamed the Central Treaty Organization.

The secret of finding one's way through the maze of initials is to use a little method. For example, begin with the United Nations, particularly with its Economic and Social Council or ECOSOC, which has links with many special agencies like FAO (the Food and Agriculture Organization), WHO (World Health Organization), IMF (International Monetary Fund), ICAO (International Civil Aviation Organization), UNESCO (United Nations Educational, Scientific and Cultural Organization) WMO (World Meteorological Organization), ILO (International Labor Organization), UNICEF (United Nations' Children's Fund) UNHCR (United Nations High Commission for Refugees) and IAEA (International Atomic Energy Agency).

ECOSOC also keeps a benevolent eye on TAB (Technical Assistance Board), TAC (Technical Assistance Committee) and TAO which is not the name of a Chinese philosopher but Technical Assistance Operations. Moreover, it is responsible for ECA (Economic Commission for Africa), ECAFE (Economic Commission for Asia and the Far East), ECE (Economic Commission for Europe) and ECLA (Economic Commission for Latin America).

Not all organizations are so easily explained in family tone fashion. SCAR (Special Committee on Antarctic Research) stands on its own. So does SCOR (Special Committee on Oceanographic Research). Advertisers no doubt regret the passing of SUNFED (Special United Nations Fund for Economic Development) and may wonder why world affairs should be lumbered with an outlandish word like UGTAN (Union Générale des Travailleurs d'Afrique Noire or General Union of Workers of Black Africa). But matters become really complicated when two organizations pick the same set of initials. It would, for instance, be fatal for any diplomat to confuse the OAS (Organization of American States) with the French right-wing "Secret Army" die-hards who used bombs and machine guns to try to change de Gaulle's Algerian policy.

Nothing is likely to stop the flow of initials. They and the agencies they stand for are a sign of our times. The important question at issue of course is, Do they work as well as they should?

In the immediate postwar period they all experienced staffing problems. There were just not enough doctors, teachers, scientists, engineers or even administrators to go round, and countries that were busily making good the damage they had suffered in the war were reluctant to release their experts to an international organization. Those they did release could often hardly be classified as efficient or competent. The explanation was that some governments with vast war-inflated civil service establishments treated the new international bodies as convenient dumping grounds for officials they wished to be rid of.

Today this problem is less acute, but the need for striking a balance between the number of nationals from different member countries still works against a recruiting policy of the best man for the job. Balance and compromise also enter into the picture when it comes to programing and budgeting. Everyone wants a slice out of the available cake. Approval of an elementary teaching program for one country will depend on whether another government receives some agricultural machinery and a third gets radar equipment. Horse-trading behind the scenes is so intense in many cases that the casual visitor may well wonder whether there is any time left to look at the problems of hunger, disease, illiteracy and poverty from a broad international angle.

Not that it is altogether easy to discover the exact nature and extent of the problems from the language some international bodies are compelled by their member countries to use in their reports. A country may have a population that is undernourished, illiterate and living in hovels but to say so is likely to be regarded as an insult to national dignity. A development program may collapse through local inefficiency and corruption, but an international report would have to speak of "temporary delays caused by administrative difficulties." To call a country "underdeveloped" is to ask for trouble; to call it "developing" will cause no offense.

The chief obstacle to more gracious international living, in fact, is ingrained national habits of thought and action, of sensitivity and prejudice, and the way most international bodies are organized does little to overcome it. In theory, of course, most international bodies are controlled by their member countries, but senior ministers capable of committing their governments on important issues can attend only now and then and for a short time. They can certainly not control its activities in any detail. In practice, therefore, the main burden of making an international body work falls on its director or secretary-general and his staff. If he is weak and ineffective, little or nothing will get done. If he is strong and purposeful, he is liable to establish an international technocracy whose members are ultimately responsible only to their own high ideals and conscience. Neither result is desirable, and since there is likely to be more international togetherness rather than less—whether we like it or not—a breakthrough in organization and control of international bodies will have to come sooner or later.

All this, of course, does not apply to primarily technical bodies like the Universal Postal Union, the World Meteorological Organization or Interpol. It may not even matter much in the case of organizations like UNESCO, but it does matter in ventures like E.C.S.C. (European Coal and Steel Community) and E.E.C. (European Economic Community), which affect the lives of millions. In both cases a council of ministers from each of the member countries decides top policy questions; but since the ministers inevitably have to face many other demands on their time, and a host of the decisions that have to be made are of a highly complex nature, E.C.S.C.'s and E.E.C.'s permanent and extremely competent staffs have in fact become the pace-setters. In both cases, too, there are assemblies drawn from the parliaments of the member countries, but their power of demanding the dismissal of

E.C.S.C.'s High Authority or E.E.C.'s Commission is limited. In any case, they can only have their say after and not before the High Authority or the Commission have acted.

Curiously enough, the pilot project in this novel form of international cooperation, E.C.S.C., has its head-quarters in the tiny Grand Duchy of Luxembourg, which affords those with a nostalgic hankering for the diplomatic ways of former days an excellent opportunity to compare the old and the new. The High Authority's offices over-look the ancient fortress town.

A businessman recently visiting there found a sizeable crowd outside his hotel when he was driven back in a shining, black E.C.S.C. limousine. A Luxembourg officer, resplendent in full dress uniform, rushed up to open the door; and as he stepped out, a group of officers, standing by the hotel entrance, saluted smartly. The ornate hotel lobby was crowded with men and women in full evening dress.

The porter informed him proudly, "Her Royal Highness the Grand Duchess is giving a State Dinner to His Excellency the Chancellor of Austria," adding discreetly, "Her own palace isn't large enough for big occasions like this."

To the businessman it seemed as if he had suddenly stepped back into the world of Metternich and the gay, dancing Congress of Vienna. Turning to a friend, he said a little sadly, "The future may belong to things like the European Coal and Steel Community, but is there ever likely to be a film called "The E.C.S.C. Dances?"

16:

Of Interpreters
and Translation
Systems

CERTAINLY THERE IS NO LACK OF SIR WINSTON CHURCHILL'S diplomatic "jaw-jawing" at the present time. The difficulty is that every statesman these days insists on jaw-jawing in his own language—which means that he is almost entirely dependent on the skill and expertise of a professional interpreter to get his message across.

It is a situation that irks and irritates some public men. In 1944, for instance, when Sir Winston Churchill visited Paris shortly after the liberation of the city, the French crowds clamored for a speech. British army headquarters at once put their best linguists at Sir Winston's disposal, but he impatiently brushed aside their offers of

211

help and strode out onto the balcony of the Hotel de Ville with measured, determined steps. *"Prenez garde!"* he exclaimed menacingly; and: when there was complete silence in the square below he added in his best conspiratorial manner, *"Je vais parler français."* His audience went delirious and for the rest of the speech seemed to be blissfully oblivious of Churchill's cavalier treatment of French syntax and pronunciation.

Admittedly, Sir Winston's determination to act as his own interpreter did not always meet with such happy results. At a big British military parade a group of distinguished French guests were puzzled and shocked when Britain's war leader pointed to a contingent of ATS, the British equivalent of the American WACs, and proudly announced, *"Voilà, le Service Volontaire Féminin pour l'armée."*

The reason, however, why more men in the public international eye do not follow Sir Winston's example and gaily plunge into languages other than their own, is not fear of committing linguistic faux pas but national prestige. Most Soviet diplomats speak excellent English, but none of them would dream of addressing the United Nations in that tongue. To do so would in their view be tantamount to acknowledging Anglo-American supremacy.

Diplomats in the Middle Ages were not troubled by such considerations. They conducted their business in Latin, and when Latin fell from use in the middle of the seventeenth century, its place as the world's diplomatic language was taken by French. Every diplomat was expected to read, write and speak it as well as his mother tongue. It reigned supreme and unchallenged until, after

America's emergence as a world power in this century, it had to accept English and later, after the Second World War, Russian, as an equal.

Today there is no acknowledged diplomatic language. Every one uses his own, wherever and whenever possible. Indeed, to do so is regarded almost as a sign of "having arrived," internationally speaking, a symbol of independence and nationhood, like having a flag or a national anthem.

Consequently, most large international gatherings tend to be somewhat confusing. To avoid complete chaos, the organizers in most cases insist on a restricted number of "official" languages. Their criterion is quite simple: if a country is big and important, its language is automatically "official." Not that this device deprives the representatives of small countries with "unofficial" languages of the privilege of addressing the conference in their own tongue. The only inconveniences it imposes on them are that their speeches will be translated consecutively and not simultaneously and that none of the conference documents will appear in their language, both facilities being reserved for "official" languages.

Since many international gatherings have as many as four or five "official" languages, the burden thrown on interpreters and translators is still extremely heavy. They, in fact, play a key role in international relations. If they do their job well, they can help to bring about a genuine meeting of minds. If badly, they can cause endless mischief. During a delicate stage of the negotiations to resolve a crisis in the Far East, the interpreter almost succeeded in bringing the talks to a stop when he translated a reference by the Soviet delegate to "the puppet regime of Chiang Kai-Shek" as "Chiang Kai-Shek's scarecrow regime."

And when President Tshombe, who speaks French but not English, and the commander of the Irish United Nations troops, who has no French, met in October, 1961, to discuss the conditions under which some Irish soldiers were being held prisoner by Tshombe's men, the two would have been better off without their interpreter. The Irishman asked that his men should be given facilities for taking some exercise. President Tshombe replied that until he and the United Nations had reached agreement on an exchange of prisoners, all the Irish had to do was to keep calm. This was translated as, "He says you must not make trouble." The Irishman flushed angrily and said that he did not want to make trouble, that neither he nor his men had ever made trouble and that when they had fought the Katangese, they had fought only because they had been forced to in self-defense. President Tshombe, who was at that time claiming that the United Nations had no right to be in Katanga at all, had that translated for him as, "They fought only in defense of their legal rights." At that point Tshombe stomped out, and the meeting broke up.

Not all misinterpretations have such unfortunate consequences. Nothing caused more merriment in a particularly grim and dreary disarmament conference than a translation which had one of the speakers appealing solemnly for "the regulation, limitation, reduction and ultimate abolition of arguments" instead of armaments. And the proceedings became positively hilarious when another speaker was rendered as having said that peace would be secured only by "pacts of mutual nonassistance and aggression."

The United Nations tries to eliminate slips in translations of all kinds by having a second interpreter stand by and listen to the translation of the first. But even that precaution does not always make for foolproof interpretation.

During a discussion on help for underdeveloped countries, an American delegate drew attention to the connection between health problems and the provision of privies. The interpreter who was translating the delegate's observations into French obviously had no idea what a privy was. He translated it as "private law." His colleague immediately spotted his mistake and passed him a note with just two letters on it—"W.C." The first interpreter glanced at it, smiled indulgently, scribbled a few words in reply and passed it back. "You run along," his astonished colleague read. "I'll be all right."

Undoubtedly the toughest test for an interpreter is simultaneous translation. He must not only be faithful to what the speaker says but also keep up with him. Once he has to go back to correct himself, he is lost. His rendering will come over the earphones in a disjointed jumble of words.

There are only about one hundred twenty interpreters in the whole world who can successfully tackle this exacting job, and over half of them are employed by the United Nations. They have all had a long and meticulous training and passed through grueling tests. Even after that they have had to serve an apprenticeship of doing written translation work before they are let loose in the conference chamber itself to do first consecutive, and finally simultaneous, translations.

Many interpreters, of course, never rise to these heights, and even those who do, admit that their training never ends. "A good interpreter," one of them explains, "must know almost as much about world affairs as the statesmen whose speeches he translates. Otherwise he will miss subtle but significant references to events in some distant part of the world or ignore nuances which may herald a change of attitude on the part of the government which the speaker represents. He must study the great international figures, because he will be translating them time and again. The more he can learn about their mannerisms, their turns of phrase, their cast of mind, the better he will do his job."

Many top-notch interpreters, in fact, know the world's great so well that they can often tell after the first minute or so whether a speech is going to be conciliatory, aggressive or noncommittal. They also have no illusions about the oratorical pretensions of the high and mighty. "We have heard most of it before," they point out, "even the jokes."

Boredom, indeed, is one of the occupational hazards of the job, for a bored interpreter easily becomes careless; and carelessness, whether in oral or written translations, can have entirely unforeseen consequences, even if no more than one word is involved.

In 1954 the Soviet Union proposed to the United States that the two countries should conclude a mutual security treaty and submitted two draft texts, one in English and one in Russian. Mr. Charles Bohlen, who was then United

States ambassador in Moscow, went over the two drafts line by line and discovered that the English version prohibited the U.S. and the U.S.S.R. from "entering" any alliance of which the other was not a member while the Russian text used the word "participating." According to the English version the United States could have remained a member of NATO because she was already in it and would not be "entering." According to the Russian text, however, she would have had to leave NATO because she had bound herself not to "participate" in an alliance to which the Soviet Union did not belong.

Officials concerned with running mammoth international get-togethers like the United Nations hope to be able to ease the burden of interpreters in the not too distant future, at least as far as written translations are concerned. They have their eye on the translation computers which are being developed by a number of adventurous electronics companies, but unfortunately none of the models seems to be entirely satisfactory yet.

When one machine was recently instructed to translate the phrase "Out of sight, out of mind" from English into Russian, it came up with "Invisible and insane." And "The spirit is willing but the flesh is weak" in English emerged in Russian as "The whisky's all right, but the meat has gone bad."

217

17:

The Atlantic Alliance

THE ATLANTIC ALLIANCE BEGAN LIFE WITH ONE GREAT
advantage over most other international bodies: its members knew exactly what they wanted.

When the twelve founder nations—the United States,
Canada, Iceland, Britain, Norway, Denmark, Holland,
Belgium, Luxembourg, France, Portugal and Italy—banded
together in 1949 in a mutual defense pact which was later
joined by Greece, Turkey and the Federal German Republic to bring the membership to fifteen, the Communists
were already in control of virtually half of Europe. Since
the end of the war in 1945, Poland, Hungary, Rumania
and Bulgaria had been turned into one-party People's
Democracies. In Greece the Communists had taken up

219

arms against the government. In Czechoslovakia a Communist coup d'état had put an end to the independence of a republic that had only been reborn a few short years before. Berlin had been blockaded by the Russians and only a massive allied airlift was keeping its two million inhabitants from starvation.

The Communists, in fact, at that time seemed to be able to pick first on one country and then on another more or less at their own convenience. And although they were not always successful in every one of their ventures, they were well on their way toward gobbling up Europe piecemeal.

The process had been going on for almost four years but it needed the cumulative effect of a long succession of Soviet attempts at expansion to convince the Western powers that moral indignation by itself was not an adequate answer to force or the threat of force. If the rot was to be stopped, something more was required.

The remedy, prescribed in the preamble and fourteen articles of the North Atlantic Treaty, was simple: An attack on one, the Russians were told, will be treated as an attack on all. The trouble was that the combined forces of all the Atlantic partners in Europe were not large enough to cause anyone in the Kremlin to lose a night's sleep. At the time there were less than twelve divisions in Western Europe, most of them serving as occupation forces in Germany, where, apart from straightforward soldiering, they performed such diverse duties as re-educating the Germans, supervising the local police, weeding out Nazis and sorting out art treasures stolen by Hitler and his gang from all over Europe. Many battalions and brigades consisted only of administrative headquarters, and very few were at combat readiness.

In the air the position was even worse. There were fewer than one thousand operational aircraft, many of them obsolescent if not obsolete.

Against this ragtag band of military might the Soviet Union was estimated to be capable of fielding about 175 divisions, one third of them armored or at least mechanized, and roughly twenty thousand aircraft.

Plainly, the West needed to put a little muscle on its warning, and General Eisenhower was reactivated and despatched to Paris as Supreme Allied Commander of Europe, or SACEUR, to do just that. Field Marshal Montgomery became his Deputy Supreme Commander and General Gruenther his Chief of Staff. Below them, he set about creating a truly international headquarters. An Italian captain worked under a Dutch major, a Norwegian colonel under a Belgian brigadier general, and a British commodore under a French vice-admiral.

It has been said that soldiers belong to the only real supranational trade union in the world, but that fact alone does not explain the success, the smoothness, with which SHAPE (Supreme Headquarters, Allied Powers, Europe) worked right from the very start. Unlike other international institutions, it seemed to experience few teething troubles. Of course it had the good fortune of being given a clear and definite target: to get more soldiers, sailors and airmen, more tanks, ships and aircraft. And that at a time, only a few years after a major war, when governments in democracies usually pay little attention to their armed forces and are intent not on increasing but only

221

on reducing defense expenditures. Having previously battled in vain to squeeze some funds out of their national treasuries for this or that project, officers suddenly found that, as members of an international team, they could get at least three quarters of the money they wanted. It was a wonderful position for regular serving officers, and morale at SHAPE soared.

Naturally, General Eisenhower had a lot to do with it. Not only could he draw on the reputation and good will he had won as the liberator of Europe, but—more important still—there were rumors from the moment he arrived in Paris that he was likely to be a candidate in the Presidential elections that were due to be held less than two years later in November, 1952. The views of a five-star general, even a war hero of Eisenhower's stature, might have cut little ice with civilian governments, but no prime minister could afford to ignore the wishes or disregard the hints of a possible future President, and when Eisenhower casually inquired about the extra divisions he had been promised, everyone leaned over backwards to comply. SHAPE became the No. 1 attraction for visiting firemen not only from Capitol Hill but from every chancellery in Europe. It was a "must" in all traveling politicos' itineraries, and as a result provided the Alliance with the much-needed initial driving force which enabled the North Atlantic Treaty Organization (NATO) several years later—long after Eisenhower himself had departed for the United States and the White House—to announce proudly that it had more than two dozen combat-ready divisions at its disposal, about 160 airfields suitable for use by the latest jets, a total of 26,500 miles of submarine cables, land lines and radio links, over 4,600 miles of fuel pipelines, and storage tanks with a capacity exceeding 528 million gallons.

SHAPE was first housed in the Hotel Astoria, a stone's throw from the Arc de Triomphe and above Georges Carpentier's bar. The arrangement was not an unqualified success. "If you were a very senior officer, you were all right," an old SHAPE hand explains. "You probably had a palatial bedroom and an even grander sitting room as your office suite. But if you belonged to the lesser fry, if you were a mere colonel for instance, you may well have found yourself in a converted bathroom. Even a bright hello from Georges and one of his special dry martinis at the end of the day didn't make up for the discomfort of that."

Three months later, the Headquarters moved some twenty miles west of Paris to a sixty-acre plot cut out of the traditional hunting preserves of the French president, into buildings completed in the record time of just over ten weeks by French army engineers, and so started a bitter and prolonged feud between three small local communities, Louveciennes, Rocquencourt and Marly-le-Roi. Each claimed the privilege of being "host" community to SHAPE, not only for the honor but also for the sake of the not insubstantial funds which the French government allows communities for the purpose of "making themselves worthy of important and historic institutions which may happen to lie within the territorial limits of their jurisdiction." Louveciennes eventually won and treated itself to a brand-new sewage system.

Most officers at SHAPE were blissfully unaware of the

tense battle fought around them. They lived in a world of their own. They had their own canteens, clubs, stores with duty-free goods, and eventually their own SHAPE housing project and a special school for their children.

Not that they were entirely without problems. There was the question of food and drink, for instance. Napoleon once said that an army marched on its stomach, but SHAPE's international military staff has to march on stomachs accustomed to widely varying national tastes, and even the most solicitous planning in the Quartermaster's department did not always meet the case. In the beginning, wine was ordered for the French, beer for the British and Coca-Cola for the Americans. Unfortunately, as things turned out, the Americans went for the beer, the British for the wine and the French for the Coca-Cola. And since the French were the largest Headquarters contingent, Coca-Cola soon ran out.

Uniforms were another problem. It took some time before everyone could tell the difference between a Norwegian army aviator, a Greek submariner, a Belgian gunner, a French military policeman and a Turkish cavalryman. Moreover, the splendor of uniforms, it was discovered, was not necessarily a very certain guide to rank. In the early days a sergeant signaler received more salutes than even the Supreme Commander. Everyone assumed that he must be a visiting field marshal.

The arrival of the first German officers in 1955 caused further complications. Gone were the familiar field-gray, the jack boots and the high, stiff collars on the tunics. Few people at first knew what to make of the carefully demilitarized and civilianized uniforms, and one German colonel had the mortifying experience of being stopped by a security guard and told that everyone not on the staff of SHAPE had to have a special pass—including civil airline stewards like himself. The German, however, was equal to the occasion. Fishing his permanent pass out of his breast pocket, he announced with a broad grin before anyone else present could voice the thought, "This could not have happened in the days of the old Wehrmacht."

One of the most troublesome features of the Atlantic Alliance has been the proliferation of abbreviations and initials. NATO had, generally speaking, become a familiar household word by the middle 1950's, although a few members of the American and British public still thought of it as the name of a Japanese admiral and not the North Atlantic Treaty Organization, while the French abbreviation OTAN suggested a sun lotion to some Frenchmen.

SACEUR and SHAPE were soon comparatively familiar, but matters became more complicated as commands mushroomed all over the vast NATO area. In 1952 a second Supreme Command was created, equal in status and importance to SHAPE, to guard the sea lanes between North America and Europe. Situated in Norfolk, Virginia, and housed in a former naval hospital, its initials SACLANT at first confused even local cab drivers. Some of them thought that it must be the name of an up-and-coming French actress and were surprised to learn that it stood for Supreme Allied Commander, Atlantic.

To officers at SHAPE and SACLANT all this is, of course, kid stuff. They have trained themselves to talk easily and glibly of CINCNORTH (Commander-in-Chief

Allied Forces Northern Europe), CINCSOUTH (Commander-in-Chief, Allied Forces Southern Europe), COMBISLANT (Commander Bay of Biscay Atlantic Sub-area) COMAIRNORLANT (Air Commander Northern Atlantic Sub-area) and COMSUBEASTLANT (Commander Submarine Force Eastern Atlantic). But even they boggle slightly at COMNORASDEFLANT (Commander North American Anti-Submarine Defense Force Atlantic), and they are likely to be completely stumped by COMSUBCOMNELM/COMHEDSUPPACT which stands for Commander, Subordinate Command, United States Naval Forces Eastern Atlantic and Mediterranean, Commander Headquarters Support Activities. Indeed, the experts have had to devise an abbreviation for the abbreviation: CSCN/CHSA.

Undoubtedly the biggest fly in the ointment of international military living has been the difference in national scales of pay and allowances. While American and British officers at SHAPE could occasionally beetle off together to enjoy the fleshpots of Paris, their French, Belgian, Italian or Greek colleagues had to stay behind, unless they had private incomes. Discreet but persistent pressure from successive SACEURS has gradually led to a certain degree of "equalization" by way of special allowances, and fortunately that "equalization" has been upward.

Indeed, it is a guiding principle of NATO's military brotherhood to adopt and adapt the best, no matter where it comes from, and to reject and suppress less congenial features. The SACLANT mess in Norfolk, Virginia, for instance, is the only one in the vast naval base where officers can enjoy a pre-lunch drink. The rest of the base is dry until later in the day. "No officer in Britain's Royal Navy," the visitor is told, "can be expected to go in to lunch before he has had a pink gin or two. So we just had to compromise, in keeping with the spirit of NATO."

Not all of the Alliance's problems have been solved so easily. Once politics and national prestige have reared their heads, even military questions could not be tackled on military considerations alone. The British, for example, who had for long been the dominant naval power in the Mediterranean, felt that the command of NATO's Southern flank should go to them. The United States, on the other hand, refused to put its Sixth Fleet, the strongest naval force there since the war, under a British admiral who might possibly have little or no experience in handling aircraft carrier forces. Consequently two commands were set up—one, South, under an American admiral, and one, Mediterranean, under a British admiral. To complicate matters still further, the Greeks refused to put any of their soldiers under a Turkish commander, and the Turks any of theirs under a Greek commander, and so an American general had to be inserted into the command structure as a sort of bridge between the two. Furthermore, both the Turks and the Greeks each wanted a naval command of some kind in the Eastern Mediterranean, and, to compound the confusion, de Gaulle eventually withdrew the French Mediterranean fleet from NATO altogether.

It is, therefore, perhaps not surprising that the command structure on NATO's Southern flank looks somewhat like a "dog's breakfast," to quote Field Marshal Montgomery. The only consolation is that everyone involved knows that the whole rickety setup will be scrapped for something more sensible at the first sign of real trouble.

The job of trying to sort out these and similar problems has from the very beginning of NATO belonged to the Council of Ministers; but since that could meet only twice or three times a year, and since the various committees which were supposed to advise it on finance, strategy and policy were located in different capitals and spent vast sums on postage, cables and telephone calls merely to keep in touch and coordinate their activities, much of the real work in the early days fell on General Eisenhower.

The first Secretary General was Lord Ismay, Churchill's Chief of Staff during the Second World War and a former Cabinet Minister. Looking at the Alliance's complex committee structure, he once remarked that there was "too much harness and too little horse." He streamlined the organization, bringing many of its technical expert committees under one roof, and gently but firmly jollying everyone along, carried through the so-called infrastructure program of communications and supply without which none of NATO's commanders could move an inch.

He was followed by Paul-Henri Spaak, who retired temporarily from Belgian politics in the hope of turning the NATO Council and Secretariat into a policy-forming instrument for the whole Alliance; but Spaak discovered eventually that the Atlantic powers were not yet ready for such a revolutionary step. When it comes to questions that are regarded as being of transcendent national interest, NATO members still tend to act on their own.

Habits of cooperation have, however, developed almost

by stealth. None of the member countries want to do without NATO, and somehow sometime difficulties are ironed out, be they big or be they ever so small. Often it is the smallest problems that give the most trouble.

Take the vexing question of national holidays, for instance. Within the first fortnight of every July, Canada celebrates Dominion Day on the first; the United States, Independence Day on the fourth; and France, Bastille Day on the fourteenth. The Canadians in the Secretariat and at SHAPE naturally expect their American and French colleagues to respect the first as punctiliously as they in their turn are expected to observe the Fourth and the Fourteenth. Consequently, taking into account two weekends—which no one is willing to surrender—NATO finds its number of effective working days in the first two weeks of July sadly reduced.

This would not matter if it happened only in the first half of July. But the NATO Club has twelve other members, every one with a national day of one sort or another. Moreover, many countries also celebrate liberation days, constitution days, days of national unity and various saints' days.

NATO tried to stem this flood of holidays by setting up a committee, but a British brigadier pointed out testily during its long deliberations, "I'm damned if I'm going to pay the slightest attention to Independence Day or Bastille Day if everyone else doesn't observe the Queen's Birthday."

In the end a compromise was reached: all national holidays must be shown the same measure of respect. This pleased everyone, but as one of SHAPE's staff officers observed candidly, "After this, NATO can't really afford to take in any more allies."

18:

"Summitry"

FOREIGN AFFAIRS THESE DAYS ARE DOMINATED BY THE
twin themes of bigness and height. Our fate and that of
generations yet unborn rests, we are told, on something
called "The Summit," a kind of fairly recently discovered
diplomatic peak which, like Mount Everest, appears to be
surrounded by extensive mountain ranges, mysteriously
known in diplomatic parlance as "Little Summits," "Pre-
Summits," "U.N. Summits," "Western Summits," "Warsaw Pact Summits" or "Eastern Summits."

Nor is this all. Hardly a week passes without a report
that this or that group of gentlemen representing Powers
briefly referred to as "The Big Two," or "Three," or
"Four," or "Five" is busy scaling one or other of the
slopes of the many diplomatic mountainous ranges now
available.

It would not be so difficult to follow all this activity if

newspaper editors and diplomatic pundists could be induced to agree on a common terminology. But whenever there is a Foreign Ministers' Conference in Geneva between the United States, the Soviet Union, Britain and France, some newspapers are sure to describe the affair as the "Little Summit of the Big Four," while others plump for the "Little Summit of the Little Four."

Calling foreign ministers "little" may seem impolite, but it would at least be logical if everything involving their chiefs, the heads of government, were automatically to become "big." At this point, however, the newspaper reader finds inconsistency heaped upon inconsistency. When in 1959 President Eisenhower made a whirlwind tour of Europe to talk to Mr. Macmillan in London, General de Gaulle in Paris and Chancellor Adenauer in Bonn, commentators spoke of history as "a series of little summits." And when President Kennedy and Mr. Krushchev met in Vienna in the spring of 1961, it was pointed out that the get-together of the Top Two of the Biggest Two did not amount to a proper "Summit" because the Big Two of the Little Two of the Big Four had not been present at the time.

Yet, however confused the terminology may be—and mountaineering terms are obviously the vogue—the trend of our age is clear: diplomacy is increasingly becoming the preserve of the toppest of Top People, and lesser mortals, including even foreign ministers, are treated merely as part-time helps.

Naturally, professional diplomats are extremely suspicious of this development. No good, they argue, has ever come of top-level meetings.

232

When King Vortigern of Kent arranged a conference in 449 A.D. with the Jutish chieftains Horsa and Hengist, his intention was to secure their support against the Picts and the Scots. Instead, the Jutes seized the chance to gobble up him and his kingdom.

The only result of the meeting between Henry VIII and Charles V was that they took an intense dislike to one another. Neither could understand how, if monarchs ruled by divine right, the other happened to find himself on a throne.

When Napoleon and Alexander I of Russia met on a raft in the river Niemen near Tilsit in East Prussia in 1807, the Czar allowed himself to fall under the spell of the upstart Corsican and discovered his mistake only after the French invaded his country five years later in 1812.

The message of the professionals to Top People in fact, comes through loud and clear: Leave it to the experts, and stay at home. What, they ask, have "summits" achieved in our own time? Take, for instance, the Geneva "Summit" of 1955 between President Eisenhower, Sir Anthony Eden, M. Faure of France and the Russian double act of Marshal Bulganin and Mr. Krushchev.

It was an idea thrown out by Sir Winston Churchill some six years earlier that had started the whole business. What he had asked for was a conference "at the summit," to meet "with a measure of informality." What eventually took place turned out to be one of the most elaborately staged gatherings in history. The newspapers may only have carried photographs of the "Big Four," but sustaining these informal groups of smiling statesmen were dozens of diplomatic and economic advisors, scores of security guards and hundreds of typists, telephonists, cipher clerks, interpreters, drivers and dispatch riders.

The problems of logistics were immense. Each of the "Big Four," it appeared, required the services of three hundred men and women to conduct informal conversations with his three colleagues.

Needless to say, the preparations for this mammoth jamboree took weeks and months. The Russians, for example, had great difficulty in finding satisfactory accommodation. One luxurious villa belonging to a Swiss industrial tycoon was turned down because its oak paneling was too dark. Another was rejected because its owner was not prepared to move his gardener out of the cottage in the grounds, and when an embarrassed Swiss official explained that moving people against their will was very difficult in a country like Switzerland, the blunt Soviet rejoinder was, "This is no time for jokes." When a suitable villa was eventually discovered, the Russians insisted on being allowed to move in their own "gardeners" and "groundsmen."

None of this could dampen the enthusiasm of the representatives of the world's press and radio—over two hundred in number—who came to cover the event. They were there to report on every move; but since they were not permitted to sit in on the top-level meetings, they had to rely on such briefings as the official spokesmen of the "Big Four" cared to give them. Unfortunately the usefulness of official spokesmen on occasions like that is varied and uneven.

The British spokesman was usually good for a clear, penetrating and exhaustive analysis of some involved problem which looked well in the *Times* the following morning but gave nothing away and could hardly be called exciting. The American spokesman was strong on more dramatic, personalized information. He could always be relied upon to know when President Eisenhower went to bed, what he had for breakfast, and how many of his favorite golf clubs he had brought with him. The Soviet spokesman did not like being asked personalized questions. In fact, he was not very fond of questions of any sort, but he loved distributing carefully prepared and interminably long handouts which, since neither Marshal Bulganin nor Mr. Krushchev ever bothered to keep him informed of what they had in mind, seldom bore much relation to what was going on. The French spokesman on the whole tried to avoid holding briefings at all. He much preferred discussing such topics as Françoise Sagan's latest book.

There was, of course, the official communiqué at the end of the proceedings, but not even the most imaginative of reporters have ever succeeded in breathing life into official communiqués. In fact, the only clues the world had this time, once the conference was all over, were four little words which Marshal Bulganin and Mr. Krushchev repeated dreamily again and again: the spirit of Geneva. The phrase puzzled diplomats and newspapermen for months—until at a big reception long afterwards in another town a waiter with a tray of drinks went up to Marshal Bulganin. Ignoring the champagne, the vodka and the wine, the Marshal carefully picked out a dry martini. "We opened a new road to the solution of international problems at Geneva," he explained nostalgically. "It was there that President Eisenhower introduced us to the dry martini."

The secret was out at last. The spirit of Geneva, it appeared, consisted of three parts of gin and one part of vermouth.

Its effects wore off within a year—the Hungarian uprising in 1956 saw to that—to be replaced some three years later, at the end of Mr. Kruschchev's visit to the United States in 1959, by "the spirit of Camp David." The ingredients of that particular concoction have never been defined but it proved even less durable than "the spirit of Geneva." In fact, it evaporated completely in a little over six months at the Paris meeting between General de Gaulle, Mr. Macmillan, President Eisenhower and Mr. Kruschchev in May, 1960.

Professional diplomats regard that meeting as a classic in its way. In their view it confirms all that they feel is wrong with summits—insufficient preparation, lack of clear purpose, inflated expectations and too much ballyhoo. It may have been magnificent entertainment, but, they ask, was it diplomacy?

Certainly Mr. Krushchev did not seem to think so. No sooner had he been ushered into what had once been Madame de Pompadour's dining salon at the Elysée Palace than he announced that there woud be no summit unless President Eisenhower first apologized humbly and contritely for what he called the perfidy of the U2 flight.

His three fellow summiteers were somewhat taken aback. In La Pompadour's day even the most improper suggestions had been more subtle, and General de Gaulle decided to adjourn the meeting.

It was not an auspicious beginning, but there was worse to come. While the three Western leaders tried their hardest to get things moving again, Mr. Krushchev took his Defense Minister, Marshal Malinovsky, on a tour of the French countryside. They visited places where Malinovsky, then a corporal in the Czarist army, had served with Russian troops on the Western front in the First World War, and when Mr. Krushchev was shown a hayloft where his Defense Minister had once been billeted, he exclaimed dramatically, "Ah, cows below, and a future marshal above. Well, cows make excellent heating appliances. He is a true son of a socialist motherland." He also shook any hand within reach, quaffed copious draughts of champagne, tirelessly repeated the French phrase he knew, *"Vive la paix,"* and helped an astonished French peasant chop up some wood.

By the time he returned to Paris, he felt he deserved a rest, and decided to relax in his bathtub at the Soviet embassy. Even General de Gaulle, who had been waiting patiently at the Elysée with President Eisenhower and Mr. Macmillan, could not shift him from there. So in the end the Frenchman picked up his pen and wrote across the agenda of the summit that never was, "Mr. Krushchev's absence was registered, and General de Gaulle took note of it. In these conditions, the discussions that had been foreseen could not take place." The summit was dead. The preparations for it had cost nearly one and a half million dollars.

Yet only a year after the Paris fiasco President Kennedy and Mr. Krushchev were dining and wining together in Vienna, undeterred by previous failures or the misgivings

237

of professional diplomats. Summits, it seemed, were here to stay. Old-timers might regret the fact, but plainly the realities of power would not have it otherwise.

The trend has, in fact, been noticeable for years. The more complex society becomes, the further we advance in science and technology, the more concentrated political power appears to be. As bureaucracy spreads and committees proliferate, power, like a balloon, seems to rise to the very top.

There is a saying among cattle breeders that the bull is half the herd. Certainly this is true of the relationship between today's presidents or prime ministers and even their senior ministers. In the United States the President exercises the raw power of the State; Cabinet officers are merely his servants and agents. In Britain the Prime Minister was once regarded as the *primus inter pares,* as far as his Cabinet colleagues were concerned; today he is virtually the government. Nobody denies de Gaulle's key role in the affairs of France, and while Mr. Krushchev may denounce the cult of personality, it is he who calls the tune.

Theirs is the power, theirs the decisions in all matters of moment at home or abroad. And the advent of nuclear power has quickened the process. Push-button warfare is incompatible with committees. It streamlines and sharpens the pyramid of command. It reduces powerful ministers to mere advisors, and important allies to spectators on the sidelines. It leaves the ultimate power of decision to the men at the top and makes summits among the masters of the Big and Very Big Powers inevitable.

Still, there is no point in becoming obsessed with the

size and importance of other people's countries. Bigness, after all, is a question of relativity.

Even Luxembourg has had its fleeting moment of Big Power glory a short while ago. When Europe's four smallest countries, Liechtenstein, Andorra, San Marino and Monaco, held a midget summit recently to discuss tourism and other common problems, it was proposed that Luxembourg and Sark, one of the Channel Islands, should be admitted to the conference. There was immediately strong opposition. Luxembourg, it was argued, was far too big: against its one thousand square miles the four founder members could put a combined area of only 273½ square miles. (The half is Monaco.)

And Sark? It was also turned down—on the grounds that it was too small. Indeed, after a great deal of argument, the conference chairman firmly closed the discussion with the announcement, "I have been unable to find it on the map. I am quite satisfied that it does not exist."

19:

A Sub-Summit
Matter

FOREIGN MINISTERS HAVE TO DEAL WITH MANY MATTERS, not all of them of Summit importance. There is a constant stream of more humdrum problems to keep them busy; but let not one imagine that, even in the nuclear age, these are not treated with as much care and thoroughness as weightier questions.

Some time ago the British Admiralty sought the assistance of the Foreign Office in a matter which, on the face of it, seemed somewhat less than urgent. Checking over the scores of national anthems which the bands of H. M. ships must be prepared to play on courtesy calls to foreign ports, the Royal Navy had discovered that the only version it possessed of the national anthem of the Sultanate of Muscat and Oman, near the entrance to the

Persian Gulf, was a B-flat clarinet score. Could this, the Admiralty wondered, be correct? The clarinet score was dispatched to the Foreign Office with a request to investigate and, if possible, to obtain a more up-to-date score.

For many weeks nothing happened, and the admirals were just about to dash off an acid interdepartmental memorandum when Lord Home informed them of a communication he had received from his man in Muscat. He reported:

The Sultanate has not possessed a band since 1937. None of the Sultan's subjects, as far a I am aware, can read music, which the majority regard as sinful. The manager of the British Bank of the Middle East, who can, does not possess a clarinet. Even if he did, the dignitary who, in the absence of the Sultan, is the recipient of ceremonial honours and who might be presumed to recognise the tune, is somewhat deaf. Fortunately, I have been able to obtain, and now enclose, a gramaphone record that has on one side a rendering by a British military band of the Salutation and March to His Highness the Sultan of Muscat and Oman.

The first part of the tune, which was composed by the bandmaster of a cruiser in 1932, bears a close resemblance to a pianoforte rendering by the bank manager of the clarinet music enclosed with your Lordship's despatch. The only further testimony I can obtain of the correctness of this music is that it reminds a resident of long-standing of a tune once played by a long-defunct band of the now disbanded Muscat Infantry, and known at the time to non-

commissioned members of His Majesty's forces as (I quote the vernacular) "Gawd Strike the Sultan blind."

I am informed by the acting Minister of Foreign Affairs that there are now no occasions on which the Salutation is officially played. The last occasion on which it was known to have been played at all was on a Gramaphone at an evening reception given by the Military Secretary of the Sultan, who inadvertently sat on the record afterwards and broke it.

This meant that the Admiralty's register of national anthems remained incomplete, but as one naval type remarked admiringly, "They do write good letters in Muscat."

243

20:

A Final
Word

THE AGE OF THE "GREAT AMBASSADORS," IT IS OFTEN
pointed out, is over. Jet air travel, the telegraph and the
telephone, so the argument runs, have reduced ambassadors to the humiliating position of glorified errand boys.

Like many sweeping generalizations, these assertions
do not altogether accord with the facts. In the first place,
it was only a tiny handful of ambassadors who were bold
enough in the seventeenth, eighteenth and nineteenth
centuries to take advantage of the slowness of communications with the head office to devise and carry out policies
on their own initiative. The vast majority asked for
instructions from home in every instance, knowing that it
would be weeks or months before a reply could arrive and
that the conditions and circumstances with which the

instructions were supposed to deal would almost certainly have changed in the meantime. It was all a splendid excuse for doing nothing.

In the second place, although no government in the thermonuclear age can allow its ambassadors the luxury of going into the policy-making business on their own, the awful consequences of a miscalculation—of a wrong decision, based on a false analysis — have actually enhanced the role of the diplomat. President Kennedy has repeatedly called back his ambassador in Moscow to sit in on critical policy decision meetings at the White House. Thanks to the speed of jet travel, the ambassador can be back at his post in a couple of days.

Again, during the Cuban crisis in 1962, the United States ambassador in Moscow was one of the main communications links between the White House and the Kremlin. And even in less trying and exciting moments, both Mr. Krushchev and President Kennedy like to deal directly and personally with the ambassadors accredited to their countries. The same is true of President de Gaulle and Mr. Macmillan.

Much, therefore, depends on the personality and ability of ambassadors. They must or should be close to the top policy makers of their own countries if they are to present their nations' cases effectively, and if they are to supply their home governments with the information and advice necessary for policy decisions. They must or should possess a sure grasp of the political, economic and social forces at work in the country to which they are accredited. In the 1930's many diplomats, both professional and amateur, failed to appreciate the true nature of Hitler

Germany. For a long time after the Second World War the United States State Department had little or no idea of what was really afoot in Latin America, and throughout the 1950's the British Foreign Office badly underestimated the drive and tenacity of purpose behind the unification of Western Europe.

The gathering of information, the analyzing and evaluating of it and advizing on possible courses of action, are diplomatic functions that are more important today than ever. The newspapers and television provide no alternative. They may educate, stimulate and entertain, but no one would suggest that a president or prime minister should base his decisions on a television current affairs program, which has had to be put together in a limited space of time and on a limited budget. Even the most distinguished newspaper columnist would agree that an occasional exclusive interview with one of the world's high and mighty is no substitute for the continuous contact an ambassador enjoys with the top people in the government of the country where he is stationed.

To fulfill their information-gathering duties, many embassies have grown to enormous proportions, with specialist attachés for practically everything under the sun from culture to labor relations and science. The smaller countries naturally find it very difficult to keep up with the diplomatic Joneses in this respect. A reporter who telephoned one of the New African embassies in Washington some time ago and asked to be put through to the press attaché was told, "Press attaché? I'm afraid we haven't anything as grand as that. This is the ambassador speaking."

Diplomacy, in fact, like everything else these days, is going up in price, and the poorer countries are having difficulties in making ends meet. One chargé d'affaires in Bonn is setting Tanganyika back over $25,000 dollars a year, and the Somali Republic has discovered that an ambassador in the United States with only one other diplomat on his staff is costing nearly $100,000. With many Afro-Asian countries concentrating their main diplomatic activity at the United Nations, it will certainly become world diplomacy's main exchange, whether it develops into some form of effective world authority or not.

Indeed, internationalism and interdependence are in the air. The development of the thermonuclear weapons and the demands of trade and economics make it impossible to tackle the problems of our age in terms of over five-score independent sovereign nation states. The United Nations, the Common Market, the Atlantic Alliance and the untidy collection of international agencies are all evidence of this trend, but the exact pattern of international relations—if we avoid nuclear war—is not yet clear. Certainly the people who are helping to evolve the pattern, and who will eventually have to make it work, are our diplomats.

It can hardly be called an errand boy's job.

The Author

CHARLES ROETTER was educated at Merchant Taylors' School and the Universities of London and Cambridge, and his wife is Barbara Johnson, daughter of Sir Henry Johnson, Baronet. Mr. Roetter served with the Political Intelligence Department of the British Foreign Office during World War II. Since the war, as a political commentator, producer of current affairs programs, and regular contributor to British Journals, he has covered many of the important diplomatic events in Europe and the United States (where he has twice been a guest of the State Department) and behind the Iron Curtain.

Now broadcasting regularly and frequently on current affairs from London, Mr. Roetter has written for *Reader's Digest* and is the author of *Fire Is Their Enemy* and co-author of *Meet the British* (with Emily Hahn) and *The Wit of Winston Churchill* (with Geoffrey Willars).